Come Into the Circle

Come Into the Circle

Worshiping with Children

Michelle Richards

SKINNER HOUSE BOOKS

BOSTON

Copyright © 2008 by Michelle Richards. All rights reserved. Published by Skinner House Books, an imprint of the Unitarian Universalist Association of Congregations, a liberal religious organization with more than 1,000 congregations in the U.S. and Canada. 25 Beacon Street, Boston, MA 02108-2800.

Printed in the United States.

Cover design by Bruce Jones / Text design by Suzanne Morgan

978-1-55896-533-1
ISBN 1-55896-533-5

10 09 08 / 5 4 3 2 1

Library of Congress Cataloging-in-Publication Data

Richards, Michelle.
    Come into the circle : worshiping with children / Michelle Richards.
        p. cm.
    ISBN-13: 978-1-55896-533-1 (pbk. : alk. paper)
    ISBN-10: 1-55896-533-5 (pbk. : alk. paper) 1. Children in public
worship—Unitarian Universalist churches. 2. Unitarian Universalist
Association. 3. Worship programs. I. Title.

BX9853.R53 2007
264'.091320083—dc22
                                    2007031470

We gratefully acknowledge permission for the following: "Earth Mother, Star Mother" by Starhawk © 1991 by Starhawk (www.starhawk.org); "As I Grow and Learn" from *A Book of Pagan Prayer* by Ceisiwr Serith with permission of Red Wheel/Weiser (to order call 1-800-423-7087); prayers by Kevin Morais reprinted with permission of Kevin Morais and The World Prayers Project (www.world-prayers.org); Jewish prayer ("Grant us the ability...") reprinted with permission of the U.S. Interreligious Committee for Peace in the Middle East (usicpme@aol.com); "Water Runs Deep," from *Present Moment, Wonderful Moment: Mindfulness Verses for Daily Living* (1990, 2007 rev. ed.) by Thich Nhat Hanh with permission of Parallax Press, Berkeley, California (www.parallax.org); "Prayer of Gratitude" © Abby Willowroot, reprinted with permission of Abby Willowroot; reading by Robert T. Weston reprinted with permission of Dick Weston-Jones; reading by Mark Mosher DeWolfe reprinted with permission of William DeWolfe and Barbara DeWolfe; Max Coots, Jackie Creuser, Tim Haley, O. Eugene Pickett, Barbara J. Pescan, Ruth Gibson, Frances Reece Day, Beth Casebolt, Richard Gilbert, Martha Munson, Marjorie Montgomery, Gary Kowalski, Joel Miller, Connie Barlow,

Continued on page 251

For Becky,
her little light still shines
in the hearts of those of us who love her

Contents

Introduction   ix

What Children Need from Worship   1
Workshop on Setting Worship Goals   13
Target Audience   21
Styles of Worship   27
Creating a Framework   35
Considering Content   41
Ritual   51
Music   59
Stories and Mini-Sermons   67
Meditation and Prayer   73
Themes   83
Intergenerational Worship   89
Conclusion   97

Child-Friendly Worship Resources   99

    Chalice Lightings and Opening Words   101
    Spoken Meditations   113
    Guided Meditations   127
    Prayers   135
    Responsive Readings and Litanies   149
    Stories   175
    Mini-Sermons   189
    Songs   201
    Closing Words   205
    Orders of Service   215

For More Information and Ideas   219
Multicultural Resources   245

Introduction

I wish that everyone could experience what it's like to sit in the leader's chair during a children's worship service. Then they could see what I do on Sunday mornings—the wonder on the small faces as we sing our opening song or perform hand motions for the chalice lighting. Everyone could witness the small bundles of energy quiet themselves for the guided meditation or listen in rapt wonder to the story.

When we worship with children, simple moments are brought to life as we see them anew through the perception of a child. Youngsters in church often experience magic in the ordinary, gaining a new sense of the specialness of life.

In worship, children openly share their spiritual natures with each other. As we give them the time and space to participate in their own worship service, we offer them a chance to build connections and affirm their need to celebrate life.

At home recently I was reminded yet again of how children can appreciate the special and sacred moments of daily living that the rest of us so easily overlook. On bright summer mornings, the sun shines directly into the windows of our family room. Through the various prisms hanging there, rainbows are projected onto the walls and floor. This has become such a routine occurrence for me that many mornings go by without me even noticing the rainbows. My children, however, never fail to notice.

The other day we were rushing out the door for an early appointment, and I was eager to get the children ushered out to the garage as soon as possible. But as soon as we hit the family room, I heard the gasps and shrieks of, "Look Mom!"

I nearly groaned. We were already late. The last thing we needed was one more delay in our chaotic dash out the door.

But I looked. There, on the carpet, in the spot where I had been just about to step, was a beautifully arched rainbow—fully formed and intensely shimmering—so bright you could distinctly see each of the seven bright colors which curved together so perfectly. To think I came so close to missing it, ignoring it, almost stepping on it. In my hurry to rush into the business of life, I nearly missed a chance to catch a glimpse of its beauty.

Sometimes it takes the perspective of a child to call our attention to the really important things in life—like rainbows—which are there for such a short time before disappearing forever.

This kind of attention to the beauty all around us is much like an appreciation of the holy. Effective worship for children incorporates the natural awareness of children. It provides a special experience for youngsters aimed at their particular needs and interests. In this way, the worship affirms the particular perspectives of children and meets them where they are, something we all need in our spiritual lives.

Planning worship from a child's perspective is also a good way to help our children feel part of the church. When a Unitarian Universalist congregation sends the message that they believe in the inherent worth of all people, no matter what their age, children come to believe that they are an essential piece of that community. For worship not only helps develop a sense of personal spirituality, it helps children establish connections with one another. Children build relationships in church that are of a different order from those in most other settings.

Good children's worship can also help our young ones understand the importance of developing and expressing their faith. When this is affirmed, children establish a strong sense of religious identity. The church becomes an important part of their lives and who they are. Worship can create a sense of truly belonging to a religious community; it can also be the catalyst for spiritual growth and the inspiration children need for faith development.

My goal is to explore the process by which this takes place and to share some resources for worshiping with children. Young people have unique needs and a desire to explore their spiritual natures with trusting, caring adults. Recognizing that many people have not experienced a moving and effective children's worship at a Unitarian Universalist congregation, I often start with references to worship aimed at adults—assuming that readers have experienced such services. Once the common reference point is established (how the elements build upon one another, the power of music, etc.), then these same concepts are considered in light of creating meaningful services for children.

The first part of this book is designed as a guide for developing and leading a children's worship service, with information about the spiritual development of children and their unique needs. The second part offers resources for worship leaders, including an assortment of chalice lightings, opening and closing words, meditations, prayers, and litanies arranged by theme according to the Unitarian Universalist Principles and the Sources of our living tradition. Also provided is a collection of stories and mini-sermons which can be used in worship with children, as well as some sample orders of service. The resources are culled from the files of many of my colleagues throughout our religious tradition. They represent a kind of collective wisdom from successful worship across the continent, a treasury of readings that have worked well for professional religious educators over the years.

It may be all too easy for us as adults to overlook the beauty and magic of a shimmering rainbow. Or perhaps to dismiss the sight as merely a physical manifestation of light refracted into component colors, revealing various wavelengths of the light spectrum. Allowing ourselves to suspend our thinking and processing minds—even if only briefly—can give us a chance to glimpse the spirituality of a moment which children so easily accept.

Seeing ordinary moments through the eyes of a child is the real beauty of worshiping with children. Experiencing the sacred amid the commonplace allows for a new sense of spiritual awareness.

Children's worship means cultivating relationships and building connections. It means lighting a chalice, singing songs, and centering ourselves with meditation. It means experiences—memorable, mystical, and magical—that stir their hearts and their expanding minds. It means reaching for rainbows, and even, if only spiritually, touching them.

What Children Need from Worship

Children are spiritual by nature. They haven't yet lost their sense of awe, mystery, and reverence for the ordinary things in life. Children need safety and consistency to express that spirituality; they also need a solid foundation in a rapidly changing world that they cannot control. In designing worship experiences for children, it is important to keep in mind their inherent spirituality and their need for rituals that deepen their faith and tie them to a religious community.

Children's spirituality develops and grows as they do, helping them form an understanding of who they are as individuals, what their purpose in life is, and how they fit in with the greater world. Their innate sense of curiosity and wonder and their ability to love unconditionally and fully experience life need to be nurtured so they can develop a deep sense of their faith and beliefs.

Although this book deals primarily with worship geared toward preschool- and elementary school-age children, it is helpful to understand some additional stages of faith development. Learning about the complete process makes it easier to facilitate a stable and enriching journey through the early years.

The Preschool Years

The development of a child's faith is a fluid, flexible process. In their early years, children are drawn to the wonder, magic, and mystery of life. At this time, their parents are the greatest influence on their theological beliefs; during this stage of their development, they have *caught* their religious beliefs from the parental figures in their life. They need to know what their parents think and believe, and they need rituals to ground them in their faith.

Because they feel that so much of the world is beyond their control, and their place within it is so small (especially when everyone else seems so big), they need consistency and order. They need times which they can rely upon, when they know what is coming next. The rituals of their religion help them to deepen their spirituality by giving them a sense of safety and order in the world. By knowing what comes next and anticipating it, they gain a sense of control over the world. And this safety and control helps to nurture their spirituality so their faith development can grow along with their minds and their bodies.

According to Dr. James Fowler, psychologist and author of *Stages of Faith: The Psychology of Human Development and the Quest for Meaning*, children of preschool age unquestioningly assume that their own experiences and perceptions represent the only possible perspective. Their powerful imaginations can be encouraged through the use of stories that illustrate unfamiliar world views of others, helping children move beyond the assumption that everyone sees things the way they do.

In her book, *Joining Children on the Spiritual Journey: Nurturing a Life of Faith*, Catherine Stonehouse contends that children "simply internalize their perceptions and activities as mental pictures of their experiences." Their brains do not make connections through rationalizing or conceptualizing as adults' brains do. If the learning experience is thought of as a mosaic, children might see the various colors or even be able to pick out shapes, but they would be unable to see how the colors and shapes come together to create an overall image. Asking open-ended questions after a story can help young children learn to make those connections and understand what they mean for their own lives.

The Elementary School Years

As children grow and become more concrete thinkers, they begin questioning things. Their growing desire to determine what is real and what is not promotes the transition into the next stage of their faith development. They begin to have a strong need to know not just what their parents think and believe, but why. They now feel there must be a reason why things are the way they are and why things are done in a certain way. Their central task during this period of spiritual development is to sort the real from the unreal, to determine what is make-believe and what is fact.

In his work with children, psychiatrist Dr. Robert Coles discovered that children become immersed in the religious life of communities that nurture their spiritual growth. It is here that they are introduced to the religious symbols, rituals, traditions, stories, and elementary theologies of their culture. In his book, *The Spiritual Life of Children*, Dr. Coles stresses that this religious indoctrination occurs even in children who are raised in overtly secular or blatantly anti-religious environments. This is because religious symbols and language are so widely present in this society that virtually no child reaches school age without having constructed—with or without religious instruction—an image or images of God.

School-age children's religious beliefs are absorbed from the influential adults they see as authorities to whom they can look for answers: their parents, their teachers at school, and their religious education teachers at church. During this stage in their faith development, they are *taught* their religion by the important people in their lives.

At this time, it is important for them to begin understanding the specifics of what distinguishes their religion from others. Elementary school-age children need a chance to begin forming questions in their minds and looking for authorities in the world around them. They are looking for ways to experience the specialness of life, to learn why the central rituals of their religion are important, and to consider the specific content of those rituals. They need a sense of what makes their religion special or unique, yet they must be presented with ideas that stretch that concrete thinking into a deeper understanding to help them progress to the next level.

The development of a deep sense of fairness and justice has a strong influence on elementary school-age children's spirituality. They appreciate the themes of right and wrong and like to experience morality plays in their worship. They also like the comfort provided by the rituals of worship, not just for the sake of consistency, which is important for the younger child, but because it gives them a sense of order, which is necessary in their world full of rules and helps them establish a sense of who they are as religious individuals.

Their newly developed interest in narrative means stories help them feel connected to one another and affirm their experience. While the worship rituals help them understand the unique qualities of their religion, stories expand and deepen their spiritual tendency to make connections and understand the perspectives of others.

However, because children during the elementary years are such concrete thinkers, they interpret literally the stories they hear as part of worship and view the symbols of their religion as one-dimensional. They cannot yet perform critical analysis or extrapolate deeper meaning from the story; the meaning remains trapped within the story's narrative.

Eventually, their ability to understand multiple points of view clashes with their tendency to sort fantasy from reality, and as a result, they are forced to look for meaning beyond the story. Fowler suggests that reflection on and analysis of these stories provides the spiritual challenge for school-age children to move on to the next stage of faith development.

The Middle School Years

During early adolescence, young people can develop the ability to conceptualize a universe of possibilities and to understand different realities and truths. Fowler explains that at this age, the symbols of children's religion remain important, but the meanings of these symbols are not separable from the symbols themselves. The actual objects are considered sacred, not what they stand for.

So much of middle-schoolers' thoughts and emotions is tied to their hormones and the body changes they are experiencing. They want to be individuals, but within a group. The influence of peers and, in particular, close friends grows significantly. They are acutely aware of the expectations and judgments of these friends, and they seek out others who share their own world view. They can move back and forth between the worlds of childhood and adulthood with an often alarming speed, which can cause the adults in their lives to experience emotional whiplash.

It is at this time that many youth either buy into the religion they have been raised with or reject it as not personally meaningful. This is why so many religious traditions incorporate a formal process in which their young people study and then, as part of a special celebration, explicitly adopt the faith for themselves. If they continue to be actively engaged with their religious community, then they have *bought* the faith for themselves.

Most youth today consider themselves spiritual, even if they don't think of themselves as religious. They, like children and adults, need a safe place to explore their spirituality, suspend their "thinking" brains, and experience the power of the world.

To create meaningful worship for them, it is important to know the culture and forms of communication for their generation. While the essential elements of a traditional service (such as songs, readings, and meditation) will work in a youth service, the selection and implementation of these elements, as with younger children, must fit the attention span and interests of the group. Sermons need to be shorter and/or interactive. Songs must be carefully selected, since asking young adolescents to sing complicated pieces often raises issues of self-confidence and may result in outright rebellion. Using recorded music, particularly popular music with spiritual themes, or having youth read the words of the song as a chant can be much more successful.

The High School Years

Older youth may begin deep theological reflection, and many may even have started to apply this reflection to their lives. Their primary spiritual task is discovering who they are as religious individuals, as part of a faith community, and as religious persons in the wider world. In his essay, "Learning Types and Their Needs" from the book *Essex Conversations*, Rev. Daniel Harper writes that, appropriately nurtured, this reflection will lead to additional theological reflection, further application, and an even deeper spiritual development.

Youth of high-school age often prefer deeply spiritual elements in their worship, such as chanting, guided meditations, songs sung in rounds, and ceremonial rituals. They prefer worship that is highly interactive and that creates connections or relationships between the participants through active elements such as spiral dances. They need to be active participants in both the worship service and the creation of that service.

Designing Worship for Children

Understanding where children are on their journeys of faith development and spirituality is only the beginning. Designing meaningful worship experiences for them involves using the right elements to help create a favorable environment for spiritual development. A framework that is specifically created to be used from week to week and adapted to fit the theme of the day's worship can provide an effective way of establishing necessary rituals while accommodating different topics and ideas.

Spirituality is a very personal thing, and ideas of just what is a spiritual experience differ from individual to individual. Just as each child is unique and has unique needs, each congregation has its own needs for worship and goals they hope to reach through that worship. As a result, there is no set formula for creating the perfect children's worship service.

Children's worship may be seen as a new way, beyond traditional classroom-style religious education, to explore ideas with children. From that perspective, worship is often considered an essential part of a rotation of experiences that children are offered in a Unitarian Universalist congregation.

Whether children's worship is presented one Sunday a month for a full hour, every Sunday for fifteen minutes, or at a time other than Sunday morning, it is crucial to keep in mind that a worship service is not the same as traditional forms of religious education. While worship may be part of a lesson or written into the curriculum, a worship service is an experience outside of classroom learning. A truly *transformational* worship experience—one that takes a person from the ordinary to the extra-ordinary—involves moving the spirit and not just the mind. A participant must be engaged on an emotional level, not only an intellectual level. While a learning experience may be involved in worship, the learning comes from the process or the experience of worship.

To touch a person's emotions, it may be necessary to go beyond using spoken words to communicate an idea. Lifting a voice in song, lighting a candle as part of a ritual, or feeling a connection to the people gathered together in the worship space raises the level of the experience and creates the opportunity for spiritual development. Rather than a "teachable moment" that can be used for communicating important lessons of life, a transformational worship service is an experience of entering into a space of sacred time and place for a moment before returning once again to the world with all its imperfections.

Sacred Space

The place where children's worship is held may dictate what can and cannot be included in the service and may even influence what leaders hope to achieve. Do not underestimate the power of physical space and its effect on the worship service or its participants.

While people can worship just about anywhere—some have transformed even dark basements or windowless rooms into meaningful worship spaces through purposeful actions—there are reasons why churches are frequently grand architectural buildings and why the sanctuary is often breathtakingly beautiful. The space a group worships in is important because it helps create an atmosphere conducive to worship. The environment helps establish the overall mood or feeling of participants while in the space.

Even if space is at a premium in a congregation, a pleasant atmosphere and worshipful environment are as important for children as for adults. We all need beauty and a space that invites us to move toward the sacred or to celebrate the beloved community we share.

Many congregations use a large religious education classroom for children's worship; however, this presents problems if classes will be held after the service. The room may have to be rearranged after the worship, disrupting the beginning of that class. Also, there may not be enough space to set up a table with a chalice and other necessary worship objects or to perform the rituals included in the service.

Since children's worship is inherently different from a religious education class, an intentional effort must be made to transform the environment (if only temporarily) into one that encourages the idea that worship is occurring and it is not the same as classroom instruction. Arranging the chairs in a large circle, designating a corner of the room as worship space, or decorating an area with special objects can transform the classroom into a sacred space. Through the creation of a sacred space, the children are given the message that this time is different from other times, and their expectations of the experience will be different.

Even decorating the doorway or opening to the room can set the mood for children's worship. As Renee Papini Cogil, director of religious education at the Unitarian Universalist Congregation at Champaign-Urbana, Illinois, wrote in an on-line forum for religious educators, "It can be magical to see students enter the room where they have been a thousand times before and see it as a new and very special place." She uses crepe paper to decorate the doorway and a support post in the center of the room. She also recommends the transformation of shared space by playing taped music or asking one child to drum softly as the other children enter the room.

Another way to transform a shared space into a place for children's worship comes from David Robinson, director of religious education at the Unitarian Universalist Fellowship of San Luis Obispo, California. In an on-line posting, he explains that children in his congregation are encouraged to create a simple barrier that they must pass through in order to enter the worship space. Such barriers can be developed with fabric-draped chairs, building blocks, or dominoes. Even the special needs of children with mobility restrictions can be accommodated through creative consideration of what such a barrier might be. For example, Jolinda Stephens, director for lifespan religious programming at the Unitarian Universalist Church of the Monterey Pennisula, California, suggests in the same online conversation that two children stand at the entrance to act as "bubble cleansers." They blow bubbles over the heads of each entering child who wants them while saying, "Welcome to our Kids' Chapel."

Religious Educator Terry Stafford uses a round rug to designate the worship space for her Children's Chapel. This has the added effect of establishing a circle conducive to building community. She also uses pieces of fabric strung across the room like prayer flags and suggests creating a special altar cloth for children's worship decorated with the children's handprints.

If a space is used for another purpose in addition to the worship service, it is important to use elements of the service that communicate the uniqueness of this event. An opening ritual is essential to let children know that this time is different from other times. Ringing a bell or chimes, striking a gong, or playing special music can signal that worship is about to begin.

Stafford's congregation used a peace fountain that was created by the children just for their Children's Chapel. After the children painted the word "peace" in many languages on the bowl, it was filled with large stones and an inexpensive fountain pump. She says, "The soft sound of the water splashing in the fountain helped make the space feel peaceful and sacred."

Due to the challenges presented by using a dual-purpose room for worship, designating one room specifically for the children's worship service is ideal. It allows the space to remain sacred and expectations to be established about behavior and attitude when in this space. A room designated for children's worship also affirms the importance of those children by keeping a special place for them to worship. They receive the message that the congregation values them and their need to worship. Once a space is established as sacred, it must remain so and not be used for other purposes or any hoped-for positive results may be lost.

A designated room also allows for greater flexibility in creating the environment for a worship service. It is important to have enough space to include an altar or table for displaying items needed for rituals, such as candles or a meditation fountain. In a room used only for children's worship, the words of songs, readings, and chalice lightings can be posted on the walls.

Sacred space communicates the message that worship is inherently different from a traditional religious education class. Worship aims to stretch the imagination, move beyond the intellect, and grow spiritually through experiences that move a child from the ordinary to the extraordinary. Exploring concepts that are beyond the intellectual level, a child can synthesize worship in a way that is fundamentally different from classroom learning.

While the service may ultimately involve learning experiences and the elements selected may enhance learning-through-worship, the process is not merely educational; it is designed to be transformational. Children need to light candles or enact other rituals of their faith; they need to feel welcomed, and they have needs particular to their age and where they are in their spiritual development. Meaningful worship experiences for children do not merely teach them about life; they help them to reach beyond and experience the power of life's mysteries.

Whether the service will be held in a space designated solely for worship or not, it is essential to consider the details of the physical environment. Ask yourself: Is there adequate lighting for the room? Does the space have a light and airy feeling? Is it possible to dim the lights for special moments of candle lighting or guided meditations? Are there large windows that allow sunlight to spill into the room but may offer views that will distract children?

The walls are a big part of the overall feeling of an environment. Sometimes a simple coat of paint is enough to brighten up and revitalize a space, making it dynamic instead of drab. If just a new paint job won't do the trick, the youth or elementary-age children in the congregation could be asked to paint a mural in the worship space. Alternatively, wall hangings of fabric or posters can be used to foster the mood for worship.

Think about the seating. Are there chairs, or will children and adults sit on the floor, possibly with pillows? Not everyone is comfortable sitting on the floor, and asking everyone to do so can be limiting for those who have mobility restrictions. A good alternative is to have both seats and pillows available, allowing participants to choose the option they prefer.

When using chairs for worship, recognize the importance of their size. Any adult who has visited a preschool classroom has felt the discomfort of sitting in a seat that is too small. The reverse is true for children; they are uncomfortable if they must sit in chairs that are too large for them. Uncomfortable children are often restless and easily distracted. Children whose feet dangle from chairs tend to swing them, causing a disruption in the worship service.

If the purchase of brand-new children's furniture is not an option, other resources are available. Many school systems hold annual auctions of used equipment, which can be a way to acquire appropriately sized furnishings at a good price. Children's furniture may also be available at resale shops in the area. Mismatched items of varying sizes, along with some floor pillows, often work better than chairs that match but are much too large for little bodies.

Finally, consider whether there is adequate floor space to accommodate the expected number of children and adults. If there is not enough elbow room, children will feel crowded and will be more likely to disturb other children when they move their bodies. It is difficult to create a worshipful environment when the children are poking or bumping into each other. Think not only of the children who currently attend but also of the increased numbers if the program grows.

If there will be movement in the worship service, more space will be needed. Dancing, yoga, and body prayers all require additional floor space for small and even not-so-small bodies to move around. Even a candle-lighting ritual or the sharing of joys and concerns requires extra room for participants to come forward without stepping over other children.

When planning adequate space for children's worship, think about the numbers of participants, the activities to be included, and any special needs, such as enough room for movement in a wheelchair or on crutches. In "A Working Paper for the Religious Education Building Committee," Rev. Eugene Navias recommends the following:

- 35 square feet per child (toddlers-kindergarten)
- 30 square feet per child (grades 1-6)
- 18-20 square feet per youth (grades 7-12)

While these figures are benchmarks for religious education classrooms, they are also useful for considering the space needed for a worship service, particularly if movement will be an essential part of the experience.

Details of lighting, seating, and wall and floor space are all important considerations when planning worship for children. These details can make or break a worship service and can mean the difference between meeting goals or falling short. They may even dictate what elements can and cannot be included in a children's worship service. Planning ahead and recognizing upcoming challenges makes it easier to overcome or work around most difficulties that arise from the physical environment.

Workshop on Setting Worship Goals

It is important for a church community to be clear about what it wants to accomplish in its children's worship services. The goals of a service determine the type of service it will be and the elements that should be included. Starting with the big picture and determining the objectives can help create a plan to follow. Once you have an idea of where you want to go, you can decide how to get there. This chapter suggests a workshop format designed to help congregations determine and establish their goals. It may be used by a task force or committee, or as part of a larger group open to the whole congregation.

While there are surely other models to help a group set goals—such as bringing in a consultant to lead a visioning process, or conducting a simple brainstorming session about children's worship—the structure of this workshop serves as a helpful guide.

Ideally, participants in the workshop will represent a broader segment of the congregation than the religious education committee. Children's worship may be a part of religious education, but it is still worship. Decisions about it should involve not only those who plan children's programming but also those who present and coordinate worship services and the parents who bring their families to the church.

The workshop will help a wide-ranging group of people to examine exactly why children need worship and to decide on its goals. This kind of input not only creates more effective worship, it also maintains continuity, clarifies values, and provides a pool of potential volunteers to help carry out the worship on a regular basis.

Notes for Workshop Leader

Before you begin the workshop, it will be helpful to learn more about the different kinds of goals that your work together may generate and what those goals may mean in terms of priorities in designing worship. For some goals, the elements themselves (such as meditations, responsive readings, or litanies) are of the utmost importance. For other goals, what is included is not as important as the mood that is created or the overall feeling that participants take away from the experience.

Some congregations feel that it is most important for children to experience the general order of worship at their church, so they can better appreciate intergenerational Sundays when they attend the main service with their families. For them the priority is to include certain key elements of the main worship service in the same general order to let children experience the style of worship that is at the heart of their congregation. For instance, if Joys and Concerns is offered at every service on Sunday mornings, then Joys and Concerns should be a part of a children's worship service as well.

Another congregation might decide that its goal is to teach spiritual techniques like guided meditation. If this is the case, each element in the service should be weighed according to how well it teaches these meditation techniques.

For some goals, however, the elements of a service are secondary to the overall experience the children receive. Instead of being selected to achieve established objectives, the elements are merely tools for creating a feeling or an atmosphere conducive to the broader goal. These kinds of goals might include helping children explore the magic and mystery of the world or helping them form connections with one another and celebrate what they have in common.

Different types of goals are not necessarily exclusive of one another; congregations usually have more than one goal in mind for children's worship. However, it is important to be intentional and to narrow down priorities, since goals establish the essential elements needed in the service. Attempting to accomplish too much often leads to accomplishing very little.

Being intentional about goals helps a congregation create a workable plan for a children's worship service that is appropriate to the unique needs of that congregation and the children who attend that church. Consider the following examples of goals for children's worship from Thomas Jefferson Memorial Church:

- to create a safe space for the children to share with one another from their hearts
- to teach compassion as we listen to one another's joys and concerns
- to make the time and space to explore big and important life questions such as: "Why are we here?" "What happens when we die?" "Is there a God?" "What is love?" "How can I make the best choices for my life?"

The UU Fellowship of Northern Nevada in Reno designs their worship for children around these goals:

- to pass on the wisdom of the ages, of the congregation, and of our program through stories that lead to small-group sharing
- to learn the songs and spiritual practices as a tool kit for the children in the future
- to present content and thus make things easier for busy and inexperienced teachers along with new parents

Other goals for children's worship might include:

- to experience the warmth of community that our congregation provides
- to celebrate special moments or everyday events that can be made special
- to experience learning in a new way
- to foster connections between the children and the adults of the congregation
- to help facilitate connections to the divine or the eternal source of life

As the workshop leader, it is important to consider the challenges and the practical matters that may limit the choices of the participants. To ensure that these goals are realistic, be sure to take into account the amount of space and time they would require.

Workshop

Materials You Will Need:
newsprint
markers
colorful dot stickers
masking tape or cellophane tape

Time Needed: 3 hours

Opening (5 minutes)

Light the chalice, sharing these words or another chalice lighting of your choice:

Come into our circle of kindness
Come into our circle of peace
Come into our circle of friendship
Come be part of our circle of love

—Beth Casebolt

Invite participants to join in singing "I Seek the Spirit of a Child" (*Singing the Living Tradition*, 338) or "Now I Recall My Childhood" (*Singing the Living Tradition,* 191).

Icebreaker   (10 minutes)

Encourage participants to share their names and the volunteer positions they hold in the church. Ask each person to answer the question "If you were an animal, what kind would you be and why?"

Responsive Reading   (5 minutes)

"It Matters What We Believe" (page 149)

Sharing Memories   (15 minutes)

If more than ten people are present, break into small groups of four or five; ask group members to share with one another a memory of church or religious experience from their childhood. (If people are present who had no formal religious experiences as a child, they can share what that was like for them. Did they wish they'd gone to church? Were they glad they didn't? What were their parents' attitudes toward church?) Ask participants:

- What stands out most in your mind?
- Is this a positive or negative memory for you?

After ten minutes, ask the small groups to rejoin the circle to form a group of the whole. Invite each small group to share any similarities or surprises that were revealed in their discussions.

Negative and Positive Memories   (15 minutes)

Draw a line down the center of a large sheet of newsprint. Write "positive" on one side and "negative" on the other. Ask participants to name a memory or thought of childhood religious experiences that came up in the earlier discussion (it need not be their own memory). Ask the group whether it is positive or negative, and write it in the appropriate column. (Recognize that some memories can be both positive and negative, and write these in the center or in both columns.) When all responses are recorded, ask the group:

- Are there more positive or negative experiences? Why?
- Is this surprising or not?

Break   (10-20 minutes)

Why We Worship   (20 minutes)

If more than ten people are present, break into small groups of four or five persons (different from earlier groupings). Ask group members to discuss these questions:

- Why do you worship? How do you worship?
- What are your favorite parts of the worship service? Why?
- Is this different from your childhood experiences of worship? How and why?

After fifteen minutes, have the small groups merge so that everyone is part of the larger group once again. Ask participants to share some answers that came out of the small group discussions. Post on newsprint some answers to why we worship and what favorite aspects of worship the group shares.

What Do We Want Them to Remember?   (20 minutes)

Invite participants to recall the columns of positive and negative experiences and how many there were of each. Ask them to imagine they have just been transported into the future. The children who have been attending their congregation are now adults and they are being asked to share childhood experiences of their religious faith. What would participants want them to remember? Brainstorm a list of memories they want children to have many years from now, and post these memories on newsprint.

How Do We Achieve These Memories?   (30 minutes)

If more than ten participants are present, divide into smaller groups of four or five. Ask each group to think about the brainstormed list of memories they want for the children and about the list of favorite parts of the worship service and the ways in which they as adults worship. Invite them to think about what a worship service for children would look like to create such memories. Give each group some markers and newsprint. Encourage them to create a picture, list, or word collage about the qualities and components of that worship service. Ask:

- How might a worship service achieve these memories?
- What would this service look like, sound like, feel like?

After twenty minutes, ask each group to share their picture, list, or word collage. Ask them why they selected what they did. Hang each group's creation on the walls so they can be referred to for the next section.

Setting Goals   (30 minutes)

Invite the whole group to think about how these images and words can be turned into concrete objectives. Remind participants that goals can be ideals to strive for, but they should also be achievable. The goals should be broad rather than narrowly focused (for example, "Our goal is to provide multiple opportunities for children to lift their voices in song" or "Our goal is for children to understand what it means to be a Unitarian Universalist.") Ask:

- How can we set goals to achieve these ideals?
- What do we need to accomplish to create these memories?

Brainstorm a list of these goals as a large group and post them on newsprint. After the list has been created, give each participant three dot stickers and invite them to "vote" for the goals they feel are most important. They can place their stickers next to three different goals or, if they feel really strongly about one particular goal, they can place two or even three stickers next to it (but they still only get three stickers altogether).

After everyone has voted, review the top vote-getters. Determine as a group which goals should be adopted, based upon votes received. Read them aloud to affirm the choices the participants have made.

Closing   (10 minutes)

Share a closing reading with the group to provide perspective and closure.

Invite participants to join in singing "Touch the Earth, Reach the Sky!" (*Singing the Living Tradition*, 301). Extinguish the chalice with a selection from Closing Words (page 205).

Target Audience

Marketing professionals are often concerned with connecting to what they call their target audience. When they determine whom they are trying to reach, they can tailor their message to fit that group.

Worship leaders also need to think about their target audience —the participants who will be part of their worship service. Decisions about who must be reached with the message or drawn into the worship experience are crucial to determining what style of worship to use and how to work toward achieving the established goals. In fact, according to Ron Sylvia in *Starting High Definition Churches*, the entire worship experience must be evaluated through the eyes of the target audience. When the audience is clearly defined, crafting a worship experience for that audience becomes a lot easier.

For preschoolers, a worship service can focus primarily on rituals and simple songs with hand motions and body movement. Meditation, if used, can be brief and highly visual or sensory. Interaction among the participants and with the worship leader is very important for this age group. They need to participate in the worship in order to feel their presence is important, so they should have opportunities to physically engage in rituals (such as lighting candles or ringing bells) and to share their stories or ideas.

Carolyn Brown, author of *You Can Preach to the Kids, Too: Designing Sermons for Adults and Children*, goes so far as to say that preschoolers respond to worship with all their senses; they don't just hear and see it, they also smell, touch, and taste it. They essentially absorb worship on multiple levels at the same time. Preschoolers respond to the whole room and the whole worship experience, rather than merely to what is said or sung at any one time.

On the other hand, when children reach elementary-school age, they become less absorbed in the total experience and begin to focus on the details. Worship geared toward them should use creation stories or tales from world religions and reflective or responsive readings, as well as a greater variety of songs because they can read and follow along in a hymnal or songbook. Rituals take on a new importance as children of this age begin to explore what separates their religion from others. They also need to understand the purpose behind rituals and to feel a connection to the other children in the church community.

Designing worship for children in middle school (ages eleven to thirteen) can focus on exploring meaning and expanding ideas as well as experimenting with spiritual elements such as guided meditation, which involves questions and searching for personal truths. New ways of worshiping, such as rhythm and chanting, can be tried out. Recorded or live music for reflection tends to be more successful with this age group than requiring them to sing songs or hymns together. As is the case with older youth, building a sense of community in worship is essential for their enthusiastic participation. They need to feel safe to allow themselves to express their individuality within a group.

Age Range

Some congregations hold one children's worship service for preschoolers through eighth-graders, and some include only children in preschool and the elementary grades. Other congregations concentrate solely on the needs of elementary-age children by offering a worship service for them, while preschoolers participate in their own worship as part of their religious education class.

The real advantage of having one service that includes a large age span is the community-building that occurs when all the children are together. However, the wider the age span, the greater the challenge for the worship leader. Since all children are not at the same level of faith development even if they are the same age, a wide age range requires reaching children on a multitude of levels and juggling interests as well as abilities.

In designing worship for a group that includes a large age span, a good rule of thumb is to try to include something targeted toward each age level's faith development. Since ritual is so important for the preschoolers, who need to feel order and consistency in their lives, it is essential to use some sort of regular ritual from week to week. Be sure to have the leader explain to the children why a particular ritual is important to their faith; this is especially necessary for elementary-age children. For example, a candle-lighting ritual can be introduced with an explanation such as, "At our church, we light these candles to remind us of our seven Unitarian Universalist Principles."

Participants of diverse ages can be involved in ways that make them feel affirmed as valuable members of the full group. Younger children enjoy passing an offertory basket, ringing a gong or bell, or lighting candles, while older children who are confident in their reading ability and enjoy speaking in front of a group can be affirmed through giving a reading. Another way to engage older children is to ask those who can confidently play an instrument to share their talent as part of the worship or to lead the group in song or hand motions.

Middle-school children are particularly sensitive to the presence of younger ones and may be quick to judge the worship as "for babies" if preschoolers are involved. They are best served by worship with others their own age (or older), unless a special effort is made to empower them in the all-age children's worship. An effective way to engage them is to enlist their help as assistants to the worship leaders. Participating in the worship as assistants allows them to be present with the younger children without having to experience it on their level; they can take part in the service and feel pride in their responsibility as role models. Worship assistants can perform musical pieces, share readings, or lead songs as they feel comfortable. They can assist the preschoolers in carrying out their duties by helping them light candles or hold songbooks.

However, the middle-schoolers' own spiritual needs must not be neglected. Even if they serve as worship assistants, it is important to include something of value to them in the content of the worship service. Their faith development at this stage involves finding deeper meaning in both the stories and symbols of faith. Thus, the leader can encourage them to think beyond the story or ritual by asking questions or asking them to help explain "the moral of the story" to the younger children.

Middle-school children need to be with others their own age to share stories and experiences; their spiritual development requires this kind of community-building. A congregation that does not have enough middle-schoolers to warrant holding services just for them should consider arranging opportunities for them to gather with youth from other congregations in overnights or planned activities.

Like middle-schoolers, youth who are attending high school have a deep need to worship with their peers. While they may also serve as assistants for children's worship services or even lead the services themselves, it is important to be aware that through this activity their spiritual needs will likely not be met, even if they are receiving affirmation as leaders and developing other skills. Arranging time for them to be with other youth (from their own or nearby congregations) is essential if they are to fully develop their spirituality.

Including Adults

Finally, in designing children's worship and determining who is to be served, it is important to take into account which adults will be present. Just because worship is aimed at the needs and interests of children, does not mean that only children should participate. Worshiping with children is a powerful experience that need not be limited to the worship leader and assistants. Some congregations have discovered the value of inviting religious education teachers, parents, or other adults to be part of the children's worship services.

Many parents like to attend worship with their children and really enjoy watching the young ones participate in the service. Creating opportunities for families with young children to worship together is valuable because so many families spend large portions of their days apart; this benefit is overlooked by many congregations. Worship services for children and their parents may be offered at a time other than Sunday morning in order to not compete with the main service. Alternatively, an additional service on Sunday morning for families with children may be held.

Even adults who don't have children of religious education age and aren't otherwise involved in their church's religious education program can enjoy the worship; they might like watching the children sing songs and participate in such an uplifting service. On a practical level, having other adults present also provides a pool of potential volunteers to help with worship should the regular leader be unable to attend.

Therefore, children's worship may not be just for the children in a congregation; it can be meaningful for adults as well. Parents and other adults in the congregation may come to appreciate worship through the magic and mystery inherent in the spirituality of young children and may receive some relevant insight for their own lives. (For information on creating worship services designed for persons of all ages, see Intergenerational Worship, page 89.)

No matter who is the target audience for children's worship—whether mostly preschoolers, a large group of children from ages four to twelve, or children of multiple ages along with their parents or teachers—the needs of the participants will determine the content and the goals. The style of worship should allow the leaders to present the content in a way that can effectively accomplish the established goals.

Styles of Worship

In creating worship for children, congregations often try to design a worship service that is just like the ones already offered, only "scaled down to size" for children. However, this concept sometimes shortchanges the very people the congregation hopes to reach. Also, children generally have an abundance of energy and enthusiasm, which can cause problems if they are asked to attend a worship service aimed at adults, even one altered for a younger audience. Ultimately, creating an entirely new kind of service—whether for children, families, all ages, or another group—presents a unique opportunity for a community to explore different ways of worshiping.

In his book *Starting High Definition Churches*, Ron Sylvia asserts that a congregation's selection of a style of worship is as important as its theology. The style of worship that is chosen for children can mirror the experience of older youth and adults in the main worship service, or it can be different. The decision depends on both the worship leader's comfort level with different worship styles and the needs of the children who will attend the service.

Educational

Most Unitarian Universalist congregations use an educational style of worship inherited from the Protestant tradition. In this style, as described by the Commission on Common Worship in *Leading Congregations in Worship: A Guide*, a speaker at the front delivers a sermon, and the other elements of the service complement the presentation. The focus is on the worship leader and the spoken words of a carefully crafted speech. The primary appeal is to the intellect and the will rather than the senses.

While the wisdom that the sermon is based upon no longer comes solely from the Jewish and Christian Bibles, Unitarian Universalist worship today remains essentially educational and verbal. This model is dominant even in services in which the sermon is not central. Panel discussions or having several readers presenting a text can replace the sermon, but the verbal presentation of material still predominates.

The primary advantage of using the educational style for children's worship is that it helps them understand and grow accustomed to a sermon-centered worship that is probably the format for the main worship service at their congregation. The main drawback of this style is the requirement for listening, which is necessary for a transformational worship experience but difficult for children whose attention span is limited.

The educational style of worship is primarily geared toward those who absorb information through listening and processing verbal information. However, as Howard Gardner points out in *Frames of Mind: The Theory of Multiple Intelligences*, many people (no matter what their age) learn more effectively through other methods, such as visual images, music and rhythms, or hands-on activities. Therefore, an educational model that is based on a verbal method of processing information falls short of serving the many people for whom auditory learning is an uncomfortable way of receiving information.

Clever worship leaders have met this challenge by incorporating visual and musical elements into the sermon-centered service or occasionally replacing the sermon with a dramatic presentation. Another alternative is to present several shorter messages rather than one long one and to intersperse the messages with songs, readings, and ritual elements that are more interactive. However, the needs of kinesthetic learners (those who learn by doing) require physical movement and active participation, which are not generally an integral part of most educational-style services.

When planning worship services for children, leaders need not feel limited to the educational model. Other, perhaps less well-known worship styles can be used and may be more appropriate for children.

Circle

Circle-style worship focuses the attention of the group on the center of a circle of chairs or participants sitting on the floor. This style usually involves substantial interaction and can be very effective for small groups as well as larger ones. The sermon (if there is one) is shorter in length and is integrated with the other elements of the service instead of being the foundation upon which the other elements build.

Because the group is gathered in a way that makes faces visible around the circle, a sense of intimacy makes sharing and engaging with one another the focus of the worship. Used effectively, this style of worship places more ownership and responsibility on the participants, who do not simply listen and absorb passively. The challenge for a worship leader in this style of worship is to create variety while keeping interactive and participatory activities as the focus of the worship.

Circle-style worship is very popular with youth of high-school age, and it can also be a successful way of presenting worship for young children. The participatory and interactive environment is welcoming to small bodies, which have trouble sitting still for a sermon-centered service. Also, the circle arrangement facilitates community-building, which can be especially important in larger churches where children attend age-segregated classes.

The circle can also be used as a metaphor for the circle of life. The framework of the service itself can be circular if the beginning and ending contain the same or similar elements. Without a sermon to build toward, the circular format gives all elements of the service equal weight and importance. (For more information on creating a framework for your service, see Creating a Framework, page 35.)

Music

While music can be a part of every worship style, in a music-centered service the music is primary and provides the main message, rather than merely complementing the sermon. For this style of worship, music is used throughout the service in a multitude of ways, and the words of a contemporary song may even serve as the focus of a short message or sermon. Nontraditional forms of music, including rock, rap, and hip-hop, may be integrated throughout.

This style of worship is very popular with young adults (ages eighteen to thirty-five) and youth (ages thirteen to eighteen), but it can also be used effectively with children. Preschool teachers have long understood the power of music and songs to help children learn and absorb information. Worship leaders can use these same elements to involve children emotionally and spiritually in worship.

Using this style of worship with children may require a leader who is skilled in music and/or comfortable performing with a musical instrument, unless plans are made to use recorded music throughout the worship. Assistants and others who perform music can help compensate for a worship leader who doesn't have these skills, but even a worship leader who is comfortable with performing and planning a service around music must also have a certain skill and "ear" for what works and what doesn't.

Relational

Another worship style that is popular with youth and young adults but can also be effective with children emphasizes sharing common experiences or even exposing vulnerabilities through relating personal stories. Relational-style worship is all about the relationships among the people worshiping together. Building community is the primary goal, rather than imparting information.

A major challenge of this worship style is encouraging the group to share on an appropriate level. Depending on the theme or topic, this may be a greater challenge on some days than others. Certain topics invite deeper sharing, and care must be taken to ensure that participants are comfortable enough with one another to accept this kind of vulnerability. However, relational-style worship need not be only about intense topics. For instance, it could be an exceptional way for people to share their favorite recipe for homemade bread and the stories behind making it. Sharing stories around the theme of bread can serve as a reflection on life and its value, thereby lifting it out of ordinary experience and making it worship.

Using relational-style worship with children can be an effective way to involve them in the content of the service without asking them to engage in lighting candles or passing offertory baskets. Children are naturally honest and like to share what is in their hearts. In fact, time after time adults have been amazed by the "truth" spoken by children who seem wise beyond their years. No matter what style of worship is chosen, throwing a question out to the participants for a response often invites a time of sharing. A congregation that is full of gregarious and wise-beyond-their-years children (and what Unitarian Universalist congregation is not?) might be well served by a worship style that emphasizes sharing with one another rather than learning lessons from adults.

Experiential

This is worship by doing and experiencing, rather than sitting and listening. Experiential-style worship generally involves hands-on activities or active body movement such as dance, walking meditation, painting, sculpting, yoga positions, or body-prayer motions. This is an effective worship style for congregations with an abundance of children who have trouble sitting still for any type of worship, no matter how interactive.

While experiential-style worship by its very nature involves creativity and expression, take care that these activities do not become simply another art project for children. Worship involves spiritual connection and emotional involvement, requiring careful selection and execution of the activities for self-expression. Painting pictures of the church building or the members of a child's family may be a valuable art activity, but is not necessarily worship. However, painting the colors that are heard and felt while listening to a selection of classical music can be a powerful and moving spiritual experience.

Celebratory

Closely related to both the music-centered and experiential styles of worship is the celebratory style. According to the Commission on Common Worship's *Leading Congregations in Worship: A Guide*, this type of service emphasizes the artistic over the intellectual, and the goal is to reflect the totality of life. Rather than create community, inspire social responsibility, or teach a lesson, its purpose is to simply reflect upon or honor life.

Music and artistic expression are a kind of celebration, and these elements are dominant in this worship style. The main advantage to adopting such a worship style with children is that it is inherently appealing; very few children do not enjoy a celebration. The major challenge is helping the children understand what they are celebrating and why. To keep it worshipful (and not simply a party at church), care must be taken to express and develop the idea of celebration and why it is important.

In determining a worship style for your children's worship, it is not necessary to focus on one style to the exclusion of the others; some of them can be used in conjunction with one another. For instance, circle-style worship might be combined with celebratory-style worship to create a service that is creative, full of expression, and festive. Educational-style worship can use music to supplement the sermon, to the extent that it becomes elevated to the level of the sermon.

It may seem like an interesting idea to explore different ways of doing worship and changing the style from time to time. However, it is best to select one style or style combination and stick with it, allowing for only a few variations. Consistency is important to people, no matter what their age or temperament. Change is stressful, and participants need to know what to expect when they come to their place to worship. Children in particular need the safety and security that a consistent style and framework offer. If variety and creativity are important to the congregation and to the worship leader, the elements within your service can be varied. This permits experimenting with different approaches from time to time, while still keeping the same basic framework and overall style of worship.

Whatever style is ultimately chosen, worship needs to create an emotional connection between the children and the material. It must offer a transformative experience. Otherwise, it is simply another educational lesson.

Using techniques such as quieting, centering, or focusing moves the experience from an intellectual one to a spiritual one. The careful selection of songs, music, and rhythmic readings can draw participants into the worship on an emotional level. Stories that are inspirational as well as affirming lift the experience into the realm of spirituality and facilitate faith development. Using interactive elements helps bring participants into the experience more fully and engages them on a level beyond mere listening and absorbing information. These are all effective ways to transform the seemingly ordinary, regular experiences of life into the spiritual experiences of worship.

Creating a Framework

One year when April Fool's Day fell on a Sunday, the worship leader offered the entire service in reverse. After the initial gong to invite quiet attention (as was the custom in this congregation), the leader gave the benediction. If this wasn't confusing enough, he then proceeded to present the rest of the service in the opposite order of the usual way, all the way up to the chalice lighting, which concluded the worship service.

Even though the order of service distributed at the door had detailed the change in plans, people were still thrown by the reversal of what they had come to expect. But that was just what the leader had intended. He wanted to shake them up in order to get them to think about things in a new way. And tinkering with the liturgy was a very effective way to do this.

Because consistency provides a sense of security, doing anything to disrupt that consistency can cause a mixture of feelings ranging from excitement to fear to anger. If the intention is to throw people off balance, it can be a powerful tool. Otherwise, it can be horribly distracting and quite disconcerting to the worshipers.

Worshipers need and desire the safety and security brought by consistency in the worship service. This is why most congregations have a framework for worship that remains essentially the same from week to week and year to year. Rev. Greg Ward, in his online article "Format of Services," points out that even though Unitarian Universalists take pride in "doing things differently," our congregations are filled with people who are very attached to the specific elements of the liturgy and their order—whether they recognize it or not.

Children's worship is no different. In fact, it is even more important for them to have a regular framework for their worship. Consistency helps bring order to a world over which they have so little control. The National Association for the Education of Young Children tells us in the online article "Helping Children Cope with Disaster" that especially during times of crisis and transition, a set routine helps bring stability and comfort.

A consistent liturgy in worship provides one element of the safe and secure setting a child needs both in ordinary life and in turbulent times. Within this safe environment, a child can be free to explore, learn, and grow spiritually.

Beginnings and Endings

The way a worship service begins and the way it ends are two of the most important factors in setting mood and establishing expectations. The beginning of a service sets the tone and creates a worshipful environment, while the ending provides the closure necessary for worshipers to leave the time of worship as transformed individuals ready to face the challenges of life.

An effective beginning invites an atmosphere that is conducive to worship. It states to the participants, "We're ready to worship now." For young children, this ritual is especially important because it helps them prepare for what is to come next. The expectation is established that they will enter the worship space ready for the experience. The beginning of the service can serve as encouragement to understand that this time is different from other times and this event is different from other events they will experience at church.

Using a ritual to begin the service is a good way to key the children in to the idea that worship has begun. Many congregations start right off with the lighting of the chalice, but many others use some kind of centering ritual to focus attention on the chalice so that participants can be attentive before the lighting. The focusing ritual might be a song such as "Enter, Rejoice, and Come In," from the hymnal

Singing the Living Tradition or another song that invites participants to stop what they are doing and enter a time of worship.

The same effect can be created by a few piano notes, the strumming of a guitar, or the playing of a short selection of recorded music. Ringing a bell, gong, or chimes can signal the start of worship, and the advantage of using these particular tools to establish the beginning of the service is that the children can participate in the centering activity on a rotating basis.

Some congregations use the striking of a chime along with a ritual activity to encourage quieting. For example, participants may listen to the sound of the chime and raise their hands when they can no longer hear it. This encourages quiet and settled bodies because children cannot possibly tell how long they can hear the sound if they are not attentively listening. This kind of activity starts the worship off on a good note and helps set the tone for the entire service.

How the worship service ends is just as important as how it begins. Effective worship requires an element to help people transition back out of the worship experience—an event that says "We're done now" or "It's time for something else." An effective ending provides closure, reinforces the experience of the day's theme, and assists in the transition to whatever comes next.

Many worship services use a closing song with a joyous feeling and sound to help send worshipers back into the world on a positive note. For children's worship, using the same familiar song each time provides a clue that the worship time is ending. Particularly when the children are leaving the worship space to go to classrooms for religious education, a song can help lead them into the next experience on an upbeat note.

Other effective ways to end the worship service also involve ritual. Using the same closing words every time fosters a sense of completion at the end of worship. Another possible ritual is the extinguishing of the chalice, which may or may not be accompanied by closing words. Some worship services end in the same way they began; for instance, a service that opens with ringing a gong or bell can close with the same sound following some ending words.

Phases of Worship

Effective, vital worship services have an order of elements that flows smoothly and eases worshipers comfortably from the beginning to the conclusion. The Commission on Common Worship tells us that worship is a form of art, an experience that directs participants through the event. It must have clear direction and touch the bases in a particular order.

In designing and presenting worship for children, leaders must consider how the elements of the liturgy build upon one another. Careful selection of elements in the liturgy that complement the heart of the service and set the stage for the transformational moment is even more important in a service for children than for adults. Because children are less able to make such transitions on their own, it is imperative to craft worship services that guide them through the experience.

Just as a tall building must have a solid foundation beneath it, a good worship service must have elements that build upon one another until the core moment when the transformative experience can occur. In the early parts of the service, it is important to create an atmosphere of temporary suspension so that participants can open themselves to the potential to be changed.

The elements that build upon one another can include readings, poetry, music (either performed or recorded), meditation, responsive readings, or litanies. The Meadville Lombard Winter Institute's "Worship for All Ages" program advises that each element be carefully selected to create an opportunity for people to "let go" and yet give order and congruence to the experience.

It is crucial that the elements of this building-up phase relate to the theme of the day's worship or work toward the message the worship leader wishes to convey. They set the stage for the main focus that is the heart of the service, be it a sermon, dramatic presentation, dance, song, artistic expression, or sharing of personal stories.

The opportunity for a transformative experience is given to the worshipers during the heart of the service. Rev. Kendyl Gibbons, one of the presenters of "Worship for All Ages," says it is the worship leader's job to "provide nutritious, healthy food for the soul." However, just as everyone may not appreciate the same offerings in a buffet, not every participant may experience a transforming moment. For any number of reasons, a particular service may not connect with an individual, but can still be worthwhile. Leaders must provide such experiences so that those participants who may be moved and transformed have the opportunity to do so.

Then, like the falling arch of a rainbow, the worship service moves into the letting-go phase. This important part of the service should not be overlooked or shortchanged. Those who have been moved by the experience must be brought back from their state of vulnerability before the service closes.

Leading Congregations in Worship: A Guide explains that an effective worship leader keeps these phases in mind and attends to the moods and involvement of the participants, and the direction in which they are encouraged to move. If a worship service is carefully crafted to guide worshipers through the experience, participants are more likely to allow themselves to relax and go along for the ride. This creates the opportunity for deeper emotional engagement and receptivity to the message of the service.

Considering Content

If you were to travel across the country and visit various Unitarian Universalist churches, you would find a wide variety of elements in the worship services. For example, some Unitarian Universalist congregations are comfortable with prayer, and participants are invited to join in a group prayer during the service. At other churches, using the word "prayer" as part of the service would be considered sacrilege. Then there are churches at which participants are invited to join in "prayer, meditation, or reflection," with the idea that individuals can choose the kind of contemplation that is most meaningful to them.

However, the one thing you are almost certain to experience at a Unitarian Universalist worship service is the lighting of a chalice. In the past two decades or so, the flaming chalice has been widely accepted as a symbol of our faith. Most children who are part of a Unitarian Universalist congregation associate the chalice with their church and with worship.

Beyond lighting the chalice, there may be other similarities among services held in different churches, but each congregation's services are unique. For Unitarian Universalists, the elements that make up the service reveal the character of the church and of the people who worship there. Since our congregations are not bound to established traditions in worship or required to present certain elements in a particular order, a congregation's liturgy speaks volumes about its character.

The framework for a Unitarian Universalist service generally includes elements that are considered important to the participants in some way. Anyone who tries to change, eliminate, or add an element to the regular framework of a service soon discovers just how significant these elements are.

The framework for children's worship should reflect the style of worship that has been chosen and the elements that have been identified as important to meeting the established goals. The elements communicate the identity of the congregation.

When selecting elements to form the framework of the service, worship leaders must be careful not to co-opt or inappropriately use the rituals or readings of another faith or culture. Such cultural misappropriation demeans those persons from whom these elements were borrowed and weakens our own faith, which is full of its own rich traditions. (For resources and more information about cultural misappropriation, see Multicultural Resources on page 245.)

Rituals

If preschoolers or elementary-age children participate in the worship service, then it is effective to include more rituals than just the chalice lighting. Lighting candles, ringing a gong, sharing joys and concerns can all be ways to incorporate additional rituals.

Some congregations use the same words every week to deepen the chalice-lighting ritual. Some congregations use a recurring reading in another part of the service. Other congregations recite the same prayer during the close of each worship service. It really doesn't matter which ritual is chosen, as long as it is meaningful to the congregation and communicates something about who its members are as a group and what it means to be a Unitarian Universalist.

Time for Sharing

Because children enjoy sharing what is happening in their lives and expressing their feelings, there is a real value to incorporating a time for sharing into the children's worship service. Most congregations that offer a time for Joys and Concerns invite participants to come forward to light a candle as they share thoughts or feelings. Alternatively, a worship leader can light the candles while participants share their joys and concerns. Other congregations prefer instead to have people share only life-changing events through the lighting of Milestone Candles.

Candles may also be used for a sharing time in children's worship services, but many adults are wary (and with good reason) of inviting very young children to light candles. Some alternatives to candle-lighting are placing a stone on a meditation fountain, holding a "talking stick" that can be passed to the child who is sharing, or passing a basket of small items (such as seashells or beads) and inviting participants to select one as they share thoughts with the group; children can then keep the selected items or place them on an altar or worship table.

Music

Songs and music are important elements in every service, and the extent to which they are used depends on the style of worship. Virtually every worship service for children includes at least one or two songs. They can be the same from week to week or can be changed occasionally. It is important to remember that the music and songs must be child-friendly. Selections whose tunes are complicated and hymns whose words are highly intellectual are not effective elements for children's worship. (For a listing of child-friendly hymns from *Singing the Living Tradition* and *Singing the Journey,* see Songs, page 201.)

Responsive Readings and Litanies

Responsive readings are a way to involve participants directly in the service and can be effective in children's worship. Generally, a worship leader reads a short sentence or two, followed by the worshipers reading a sentence or two, and the process continues until the end of the reading. This invites participation in the service and encourages better processing of the material because it is verbally presented as well as read by the worshipers themselves.

However, using responsive readings in children's worship has potential drawbacks. Some school-age children struggle with reading, and it is important that worship not become one more opportunity for them to "fail" at something required of them. Children who are not yet in elementary school are rarely able to read and may feel excluded from the process, possibly making them feel undervalued.

Clever worship leaders have overcome these obstacles by using the same responsive reading for each worship session or by having a set of three or four that can be rotated. Over time, the non-readers and children who find reading aloud a challenge come to know the familiar words and are able to follow along.

In another approach, older elementary-age children or middle-school youth can be asked to present the responsive reading with the leader. While this doesn't necessarily address those children who have issues with reading aloud, this method engages older children specifically in a worship that might otherwise be tailored toward the youngest participants. This may also be a productive way to give the younger children something to aspire to ("When I'm older, I'll get to do the responsive reading like they do").

Another alternative is to present a responsive reading as a call-back. In this model, a leader speaks the reading in short phrases and invites the children to "call back" the words right after they hear them. This is an effective way to present any long reading to children, because processing the material in small chunks and repeating it back allows for greater absorption.

If mostly pre-readers are present or if several children in your congregation experience difficulty reading aloud, a litany may be a better tool to use. A litany is not used as often in Unitarian Universalist churches as it is in Christian or Jewish services, but it can be an effective element to incorporate into worship with young children. As with a responsive reading, a leader reads a sentence or two and the participants follow by repeating a phrase together as a group. This technique allows even young children to participate in the process as they quickly catch on to what they are supposed to say and begin repeating it at the right times. This is particularly true if the leader introduces the litany each time with an invitation to the children to say the words along with the leader ("Please join me in saying our response line—'We give thanks this day'").

Unlike responsive readings, litanies do not require participants to be able to read. Participants are engaged in the worship by having to listen carefully so they know when it is time for them to add their part. Also, the repeated phrase can be an affirming sentence that may linger in children's minds long after the end of the worship, bringing back the ideas and the concepts that were expressed. Using a litany as part of children's worship can be one of the most effective tools for creating a lasting impression, no matter where the children are in their faith development.

Meditations

Meditations offered in worship services geared to an adult's intellect often include words and ideas that are beyond a young child's understanding. But meditation is an important skill for Unitarian Universalist children to learn, and not only because it is so often included as part of adult worship services. Knowing how to quiet and calm the body as well as the mind through meditation is an essential skill, and if we do not teach it to our children, we do them a great disservice.

The key to using meditation with children is choosing one that is highly sensory and does not require abstract thought. The words must be meaningful to the children and appropriate to their developmental level. A few words that are beyond their limited vocabularies may be used because it is also important to stretch their abilities. As long as the majority of the message and words is understood, then meditation can be an effective way for children to worship and develop a crucial life skill.

Prayers

Whether or not prayer is used in a worship service usually depends on the congregation's attitude toward it, the worship leader's comfort level with the idea, and the goals that have been established for worship. Like meditation, prayer can be a useful skill for children to learn in times of transition or difficulty. It can be a celebration as well as an expression of thanks. While theologies differ among individuals and families, prayer can help focus thoughts in a constructive way. Besides, while adults may have made an informed decision not to pray, children most likely have not had the opportunity to make such a choice, possibly because they (like most Unitarian Universalist children) have had little or no experience with prayer.

Prayers from many different religious traditions are available in the Prayers section of this book (page 135); they can be used to teach children about the way people of many different faiths pray. Prayer could also be used in a children's worship service as a form of highly focused, personalized meditation or a way of appealing to a divine presence. Prayer need not be gender-specific or even speak to a certain kind of divinity or theological belief. It can be a sincere wish, an expression of thanks, or a request for forgiveness. It can be a good way for children to focus their thoughts outside of their egocentric world and express ideas or concepts about the world.

Offerings

Congregations that include an offering in the children's worship service have been pleasantly surprised by the results. Using an offering in a children's service, even one not attended by many adults, is a powerful way to teach children about the concepts of generosity and giving.

While the youngest children are likely to bring money given to them by their parents for the offering, older children can be actively encouraged to save some of their own money to contribute. The generosity practiced by these children may stay with them throughout their lives. Sacrificing something for a larger good and joining together with others to bring change are powerful experiences for children. Rev. Randy Becker, a second-generation Unitarian Universalist, remembers fondly how his "weekly nickel would join the pennies, nickels, dimes, quarters and rare dollars of others to make a difference in the world."

Keep in mind that each family is unique. Differing circumstances mean different resources are available to children. To avoid any competition in giving, and to protect those who have less to offer, the best way to collect offerings is to make them anonymous. Sealed envelopes keep the money private and unknown to the group. Sending the envelopes home can also serve as a reminder of the process for forgetful children and adults.

When an offering is included in children's worship, it is a good idea to keep the money raised separate from the rest of the church budget so the children can see the pot of money grow and even help decide how to spend it. In some congregations, at the end of a church year, one-third of the children's offering is presented to the church as part of a ceremony or as a particular purchase for the church (such as playground equipment, film projector, or DVD player). Another third is given to a local charity and the remaining third is given to a global charity, both of which are selected by the children. Other congregations encourage their children to decide where to donate the entire pot of money. Llamas, rabbits, and honeybees have been purchased for families through the Heifer Project, new slippers have been bought for a children's hospital, and books have been donated to a homeless shelter, all through the generosity of Unitarian Universalist children contributing to an offering at their worship.

Stories or Mini-Sermons

Many worship services for children incorporate a story, lesson, or mini-sermon, and this can be particularly important if elementary-school children are active participants. A story can serve as the educational portion of the service in which information is offered in an entertaining manner and can be processed on different levels depending upon a child's spiritual development. Stories are more effective if told rather than read, and even more effective if they involve the participants in the telling of the tale. For young children, it is important to use books with bold, colorful pictures that can easily be seen by the entire group.

Physical Movement

Many children, especially preschoolers, need to experience worship with their bodies as well as their minds. Worship for children can be designed with this in mind, giving them an opportunity for physical movement. Children love to move in worship services; even many adults, when attending services with movement, have wholeheartedly enjoyed the experience, which contrasts with the minimal physical movement in most Unitarian Universalist worship services.

There are a number of ways to include movement naturally within a service without making physical activity a separate event in the worship. For example, during a service celebrating the earth or the arrival of spring, participants can engage in yoga poses that pay homage to the sun, the sky, or various animals. Physical movement in a worship service can be as simple as getting up and dancing to the song "Let It Be a Dance" or using hand motions for songs such as "Spirit of Life" or "This Little Light of Mine," all from *Singing the Living Tradition*.

Self-Expression

Along with physical movement, creativity and self-expression can be wonderful parts of a worship service geared toward children. Many worship leaders have come up with ways to include self-expression in their children's services. Freestyle dancing, chanting, expressing rhythms with the body through clapping hands, stomping feet, or slapping thighs all can be used to encourage self-expression and deepen the worship experience. Painting, sculpting, or creating a mural can be worshipful if the right atmosphere is established and the mood is conducive to worship through creativity. Even if an experiential-style service for worship is not used, the occasional opportunity for self-expression within a worship service for children can be powerful.

Matching Other Services

Whether or not the worship style of the children's service matches the main worship service, most congregations want to include some of the elements used in the main service. Elementary-age children need to be able to identify the symbols of their faith and the uniqueness of their religion. Thus, including some identifiable aspects of Unitarian Universalism and the particular congregation in the children's worship is paramount. Even if children generally worship in a space away from most of the adults, there may be times when they are present with their families for an intergenerational service. Having at least some similar elements in both services helps to bridge that transition and creates a greater understanding of what is done in the "other" service.

Ritual

There was a time when the deliberate incorporation of ritual into a worship service was virtually unheard of in Unitarian Universalist congregations. Because so many members and leaders in UU churches had rejected their prior faith traditions, they shunned anything they saw as "trappings" of the old religion. Ritual, such a big part of Jewish and Christian worship services, was considered part of the "old way" and was summarily rejected along with the religious traditions members had left behind.

However, things have been changing in recent years, according to Rev. Barry Andrews's essay in *Essex Conversations: Visions for Lifespan Religious Education*. He asserts that today many people who are new to Unitarian Universalism did not have a traditional religious upbringing, and relatively few come to our congregations with the sense of religious rebelliousness that brought so many to us in years past. New members now tend to be much more comfortable with religious language and the use of ritual than those who came to Unitarian Universalist churches in the past. In fact, many of these new people are unchurched, and they expect to use traditional religious language, symbols, and rituals, even if they are understood in a way that is uniquely Unitarian Universalist.

Rev. Andrews goes on to note that spirituality is largely personal and perceptual because it is made up of those values, beliefs, and religious experiences that relate to our own individual lives. On the other hand, religious identity is communal and conceptual, representing those values, beliefs, and rituals that a group of people hold in common. According to this view, ritual is an essential part of people's development of religious identity because it helps them recognize the things that are central to their faith. Perhaps this is why over the years ritual has crept back into the services of Unitarian Universalist congregations that initially rejected the notion of formalized ritual. If ritual is an essential piece of religious identity, then ritual will find itself a home wherever people are worshiping together. Meg Cox, in *The Book of Family Traditions: How to Create Great Rituals for Holidays and Everyday*, says that since a ritual can be defined as an established procedure for a religious or other rite, this makes nearly everything a religious community does on a regular basis a ritual.

Even if established ritual is not important to the adult worshipers, it is of utmost importance to children, who need to understand the specifics of their faith tradition. Many parents today understand this and seek out religious rituals for their children to take part in. According to Rev. Andrews, parents say specifically that they are looking for a congregation that nurtures spirituality, provides an ethical framework, helps them and their children answer the difficult questions of religion and life, and encourages the development of religious identity. In addition, rituals help build bonds to the religious community.

Meg Cox believes that many parents intuitively pass down their treasured traditions to their own children because the power of ritual and the need for it are far stronger than most realize. Religious families build their beliefs into every tradition, from celebrating the holiest of days to saying grace before a meal to offering prayers before bedtime. Often some of the most beloved rituals are tied to the religions of people's childhood; if the ties are broken with those faith traditions, parents are often at a loss to replace them.

Unitarian Universalist parents of this generation are no different. They, too, frequently yearn for rituals that will tie them to their religious community. Thus, parents need the rituals as much as their children do.

Being Intentional

Just because rituals are part of a religious community's everyday actions does not mean members shouldn't be intentional about which rituals they provide for their children. When most adults think back to their childhood, the moments that usually stand out are the ones tied to a ritual: baking Christmas cookies with Grandma, lighting the Shabbat candles on Friday nights, or hearing the choir sing at midnight Mass. If we are not intentional about the rituals we present to our children, it's possible that they may instead recall the rituals we'd prefer they don't remember, such as being chased away from the snack table during coffee hour, being hurried out of the main worship service so the adults can have their important time without them, or being forced to sing in front of the church each year on Religious Education Sunday.

Meg Cox explains that because religious rituals pass on values from one generation to the next, they must be intentional. Those Christmas cookies are made and the Shabbat candles lit over and over again not just because they are joyful experiences but also because they have meaning. Those actions are tied to traditions and values that are important to a family, just as receiving Communion is important in a Christian worship service or praying the Shema is key in a Jewish worship service. Rituals are remembered because they are repeated time and time again. If we want our children to remember the importance of being a Unitarian Universalist and have a strong religious identity, then ritual is essential.

Transitions

Using ritual can be a good way to mark transitions and affirm the individuals who are experiencing them. Change is inherent in any sort of life transition, be it graduation from high school, marriage, or adding another member to the family. Change brings with it stress and anxiety; using ritual to mark these moments in life affirms us and may lessen the negative effects of change. Rituals also elevate the significance of transitional moments for those who have not yet experienced them.

The Child Dedication (or Naming Ceremony) is a ritual that dates back to the very early years of the Universalist faith. The father of American Universalism, Rev. John Murray, created a ceremony to celebrate the arrival of a child into the family in response to his rejection of the ritual of baptism. In his online article "Baptism II: The Letter," Rev. Scott Wells explains that since Murray and other Universalists believed God was a loving being who would never send a person to Hell, a baptism to wash away original sin was unnecessary. However, a ritual to welcome children into the church community and affirm them as individuals was perfectly fitting in this new theology. Thus, the Child Dedication service was born and gradually caught on. To this day, it remains the most frequently performed ritual to mark a transition (besides weddings and union ceremonies) in Unitarian Universalist congregations.

In recent years, a large number of Unitarian Universalist congregations have implemented some kind of Coming of Age program to recognize and affirm children who are moving into adolescence. These rites-of-passage programs generally involve some sort of spiritual retreat, physical challenge, and exploration of what it means to be a Unitarian Universalist. Participants who successfully complete the program are affirmed in a worship service that recognizes their achievements as well as their transition into adolescence. They are welcomed into the church community not as children but as youth, and in many Unitarian Universalist congregations they are even given the option to join as members of the church with all the responsibilities that entails.

Bridging ceremonies are also held by many Unitarian Universalist churches to mark the transition from adolescence to young adulthood. At a worship service held near the time of high school graduation, youth are recognized and affirmed for the passage they are experiencing in life and often are invited to physically cross a bridge or other threshold as a symbol of their crossing into adulthood. They may be given a rose, just as in child dedications, but this time without the thorns removed. They may also be given a pair of gardening gloves to symbolize what the church community has given them: their faith tradition, which can serve as a protection from the thorns of life.

Some Unitarian Universalist churches are developing additional ceremonies to mark important transitions. Rituals to celebrate a child's reading achievement have been adopted, usually involving the presentation of a book in front of the congregation. Some church rituals include affirming children who will soon be attending kindergarten (with the presentation of an eraser to symbolize "We all make mistakes, you will too and it's okay"), moving from elementary school to middle school (with the presentation of brightly colored rubber bands to emphasize the importance of remaining flexible), and the beginning of high school (with the presentation of a compass to symbolize the concept that we all get lost from time to time, but our faith can help us find our way).

Grief and Loss

Rituals also help individuals in times of grief and loss. While any change brings stress and anxiety, this is especially true when people experience the death of someone they are close to or the dissolution of a family unit through divorce. Using ritual in these times of loss is a long-standing tradition that promotes the healing process.

When a death occurs in the lives of children, particularly when it is someone who was very close to them, it seems as if a rug has been pulled out from under them. The Dougy Center for Grieving Children's *35 Ways to Help a Grieving Child* explains that consistency and routines can help rebuild a sense of stability after a tragic loss. Rituals such as memorial services or funerals, while painful to experience, actually aid a person in moving through the grieving process. However, just as importantly, the everyday routines of life and the consistency offered by the rituals of a worship service can help alleviate the sense of chaos and disorder that follows the death of a loved one.

Divorce is another loss that occurs in the lives of many children. Judith Wallerstein, Julia Lewis, and Sandra Blakeslee write in *The Unexpected Legacy of Divorce* that children whose families dissolve through divorce are overwhelmed with feelings of helplessness, anger, and pain, even if intellectually they understand the need for the divorce (as in cases of abuse or neglect). Again, the familiarity of ritual in worship brings comfort to children whose lives are disrupted by divorce and who feel that their lives will never be normal or whole again.

Religious Identity

Even without life-changing events, children need rituals to provide a sense of order in their world. Children of elementary-school age need to experience and understand the rituals that make their faith tradition unique. They need rituals to tie them to their faith community and to give them a sense of religious identity.

Some congregations communicate what it means to be a Unitarian Universalist in a ritual using rainbow candles. Seven candles, one for each color of the rainbow—red, orange, yellow, green, blue, indigo, and violet—represent the seven Principles. As the candles are lit, the corresponding Principle is read or spoken. To help with remembering the words and which Principle corresponds with which color, the Principles can be reworded, as in this example, adapted from Elizabeth Katzmann and Rev. Meg Riley, to include a key word or phrase that reminds participants of the meaning:

Red is for RESPECT. We RESPECT each person.
Orange is to remind us to OFFER fair and kind treatment
    to all.
Yellow is for how we YEARN to learn with others in our
    UU church.
Green helps us to GROW in spirit, mind, and heart.
Blue is to remind us to BELIEVE in ourselves and our
    ideas.

Indigo reminds us to INSIST on peace and justice.
Violet is for how we VALUE our Earth and VOW to care
for it.

An alternative to lighting candles could be passing out scarves, ribbons, or flags in the seven colors of the rainbow. As the scarves are passed to the individuals who will participate in the ritual, the Principles could be read and then a parade of children could march around the worship space or even through the religious education classrooms with their flags or scarves of many-colored Principles.

Another ritual involves dropping a stone into a fountain or bowl of water. Placing the stone in the water can serve as a tangible reminder of how our actions affect others. When placed in a fountain, the stone redirects the water; it must either flow around or over the new stone, but its path is changed.

At the Unitarian Universalist Church of Las Cruces, New Mexico, Religious Educator Susan Freudenthal uses heart-shaped stones, which the children drop into a small bowl of water. At the close of the ritual, she tells the participants, "Like the water and heart stones, so too our hearts, joys, and sorrows ripple out and touch one another. This reminds us that we are all connected and that what touches one of us, touches all of us in some way."

Ritual can also demonstrate the effect of the seventh Principle, respect for the interdependent web of all existence of which we are a part. Participants can add a strand to a web constructed of yarn; the web grows larger and larger through the year as people contribute to it. This simple act is a concrete illustration of how the web grows as others build on it and what could happen if some of it were to be broken or cut.

Some congregations use a closing prayer as a ritual. When hand or body motions are added to the spoken words, the ritual becomes even stronger. Pairing actions with words helps children remember a message better than words alone.

Rev. Ruth Gibson sometimes ends her children's worship services with a ritual in which everyone joins hands as they stand in a circle around the chalice. After the benediction, participants are invited to pass a blessing around the circle by gently squeezing the next person's hand. Sometimes Gibson encourages them to imagine that all of their family and friends are in the circle. Other times she invites them to imagine that all the people or all the creatures in the world are in the circle to receive the blessings. To avoid overly aggressive squeezing from children who think it might be entertaining to squeeze as hard as they can, Gibson always reminds the participants, "Now if you should feel a friendly little squeeze on one hand, that's a blessing—a powerful good wish coming to you."

A ritual can be as simple as consistently using the same song, prayer, or response to a litany. Because the wording and any corresponding actions are the same in every worship service, the message is synthesized and retained. This makes for a powerful learning experience and helps communicate a strong sense of religious identity.

Music

Songs and music are such important parts of the worship service and the overall life of a church that their use can actually make the difference between a thriving congregation and a stagnant one. According to Ron Sylvia, author of *Starting High Definition Churches*, the type of music selected for a worship service is the most important factor in shaping a church.

Music is almost more important than theology, because it defines the identity of the church and who will be attracted to the community. When people read a sign on a church announcing its denomination, it is clear what theology the church holds. But only after the first song cranks up in worship do people begin to understand whether they are comfortable there or not.

In designing worship for children, the selection of music is even more important. Using hymns with complicated tunes and sophisticated lyrics will only result in stumbling and mumbling by the participants. With limited vocabularies, children may struggle with unfamiliar words and the meaning of the song may be lost. Tunes that are hard to follow make singing difficult for children, since so many of them can't read music or easily reproduce the sounds they hear. Familiar tunes or songs with simple rhythms are much more successful; selections with words children can understand and process prevent them from merely singing words that have no meaning to them.

Child-Friendly Hymns

A number of songs in the Unitarian Universalist hymnal *Singing the Living Tradition* and the hymnal supplement *Singing the Journey* can be considered child-friendly, with words and tunes that are easily remembered and sung. Picking a few of these hymns and using them repeatedly in worship may seem repetitive to adults, but the practice is comforting to children, particularly the youngest ones who can't yet read and follow along. (For specific titles of some hymns to use, see Child-Friendly Hymns, page 241.)

Some songbooks have been assembled specifically for use in children's worship and multigenerational settings. *May This Light Shine: A Songbook for Children and Youth* is a collection of songs and chants by Unitarian Universalist composers and is available from the UUA Bookstore. Developed through a special project of the Unitarian Universalist Musicians Network, it includes a book for the worship leader or accompanist as well as songbooks designed for children in a smaller size that is easier for their hands to hold.

A congregation could purchase multiple copies of this songbook, giving children the affirmation that comes from having their own special hymnbook. Extra copies make excellent gifts for new families who become members. With information about which hymns are sung regularly, families could use this book to sing these songs at home.

Another resource is *Now Let Us Sing! Songs for Children of All Ages*. This songbook was compiled and arranged by Phyllis Robbins and published in 2004 by Kingston Unitarian Press. It contains sixty-one hymns from multiple sources, organized around the seven Principles.

Accompaniment

A cappella singing by children can be a beautiful moment in worship, but it rarely happens unless children are particularly skilled at singing and can confidently belt out the words to a familiar tune. Therefore, to help the singing sound pleasant, it is a good idea to include some sort of accompaniment in children's worship services.

Leaders need to decide what to use and whom to recruit in order to help with the music portion of the service. Is there access to a piano in the children's worship area? Is the worship leader a competent guitar player? Are there high-school youth who are musicians and are willing to share their talents? What other music options might be available for accompaniment?

Be intentional in deciding on an accompaniment. Even if something is available and easy, it may not necessarily be the best option. The music should not only complement the songs or hymns, it should also set the right mood.

Consider the difference in sound made by an organ, a piano, and a keyboard, and the mood each creates. The organ is more formal and traditional; it establishes a mood of reverence and creates a much different impression than the more contemporary sound of a piano. On the other hand, a keyboard can add a modern element that is airy and celebratory.

The congregation's music director or choir director, if there is one, should be consulted. Even if they normally work only with adults, such specialists are likely to have ideas and resources that may not occur to the children's worship leader.

Finally, as a practical matter, consider the space that will be used and its proximity to the main worship service (if the services are held concurrently). Music from the other service may intrude upon the service for children and vice versa. If this is the case, the options for accompaniment may be limited. However, members of many congregations appreciate hearing the distant voices of the children singing while the main worship service is underway (unless it happens to correspond with the time of meditation or prayer). Careful timing and consulting with the minister or music director can help coordinate the music and eliminate distracting sounds. Anticipating such issues and working to minimize the interference and overlap can solve most of these problems.

Mood

Clever worship leaders use varying elements to set the mood and tone of the song or hymn prior to singing. Just a few bars of piano music, the strumming of a guitar, or the ringing of a bell can have a profound effect.

The mood you set can actually change the sound of the hymn; the same song sounds quite different when sung in different ways. A hymn like "Spirit of Life," for example, can sound joyful, overtly spiritual, or even mournful, depending upon how it is sung and what accompaniment is used. For a joyful sound, an upbeat, slightly rapid tempo can be used. For a reverent, peaceful sound, a worship leader can encourage the group to sing softly to a soothing accompaniment. The tempo can be slowed down slightly for a stunning result.

Different effects can also be created by singing in rounds, in harmony, or with an antiphonal (echo) effect. However, if most of the participants are young children, it is probably not a good idea to get too ambitious with such techniques. Older youth enjoy singing in rounds if they are in a group in which they feel comfortable. With middle-school aged children, it is important to consider the self-confidence issues that are dominant at this time in their lives, as well as the changing voices of the boys. Given all these issues, a more pleasing sound will probably be created if the group sings all together. With a mood-setting accompaniment, ideally the voices will blend so that no one voice is heard above the rest. This gives those children who are insecure about their singing voices the chance to hide among the crowd.

Rhythm Instruments

Music for a children's worship service need not be limited to selections that can be played by adults or youth. Children love experimenting with and making sounds. They can use their own instruments to worship through performing, thereby encouraging personal expression as a spiritual experience.

Simple rhythm instruments like triangles, bells, maracas, drums, and sticks that can be rubbed together may add a deeply spiritual element to worship. To encourage the children to match the beat, the worship leader can tap out a rhythm for the children to follow. Making their own music affirms the children as individuals and lifts the worship experience to a new level of emotional involvement.

Rhythm instruments are so attractive, it is sometimes hard to get children to stop playing them. Anticipating this potential problem can help minimize any disruptions. Consider providing a special basket and a person assigned to collect the instruments after the song to signal that it is time to move on. Alternatively, planning to use the rhythm instruments as part of the closing can eliminate any difficulties. Placing a basket at the door for children to return their instruments when they leave or inviting them to come to the front of the room and place the instruments in the basket just before they go are other ways to smooth the transition.

Hand Motions

Using hand or body motions with songs in worship helps children process the songs on a deeper level. Singing with their bodies as well as their voices can help those young children who don't vocalize well. Even toddlers can follow along in a worship service by moving their hands in simple motions.

Many Unitarian Universalist congregations use the song "This Little Light of Mine" from *Singing the Living Tradition* and develop easily performed hand motions to accompany it. Other congregations close their worship each day with the hymn "Spirit of Life," using American Sign Language motions. If a member of the congregation is fluent in American Sign Language, perhaps he or she can help teach the children and the worship leader to sign various songs; this would serve as a learning experience for everyone. The simple use of hand or body motions with a reading or song adds to the spirituality of the experience as children put all of themselves into the act of worship.

Recorded Songs

Using recorded music has many benefits, particularly if the choices for accompaniment are limited, and the recordings require nothing more complicated than a CD player. Singing along with recorded music allows individual voices to merge with the singers on a CD and helps those children who might stumble along because the words are unfamiliar.

Some recorded hymns are available on CD from the UUA Bookstore, but many of the best hymns to use with children are not. As an alternative, a congregation's choir or singing group could record the songs, which could then be burned onto a CD. If the choir members are unfamiliar with this process, you may find a youth or young adult who knows how to do it.

Popular music that appeals to the target audience can also be an effective tool for worship. With discretion and careful selection, a worship leader can use contemporary music in worship services to powerful effect. This is particularly true with middle-school and high-school youth, although recorded music also holds great appeal for younger children.

The key to using popular music in a service that includes youth is to know what is actually popular among the group. Since musical tastes vary greatly from individual to individual and from group to group, do not assume that just because other middle-school youth are enthusiastic about a certain type of music, the youth in your congregation must be. Find out what they listen to and search within that particular style or genre of music to locate something suitable.

Many songs can be used to illustrate our Unitarian Universalist Principles with elementary-school children, who have less concern about music styles and what's "in." Such songs may address the inherent worth of all people ("Imagine" by John Lennon, for instance) or the importance of taking care of our earth (such as "What a Wonderful World," performed by Louis Armstrong). Other songs that can be used for worship contain references to God or the divine (such as "From a Distance" performed by Bette Midler or "What If God Was One of Us?" performed by Joan Osborne).

Folk songs such as "If I Had a Hammer" or "Turn, Turn, Turn" (both written by Pete Seeger) express ideas of peace, fairness, and justice that can be explored through worship. Songs by the Beatles, such as "Let It Be" or "Nowhere Man," can be used to explore theological issues and the Sources of our Unitarian Universalist faith.

While the options for using popular music in children's worship are nearly limitless, it is important to keep in mind the relevance of the music. Songs should contain words that relate to the theme of the worship service and complement the day's overall plan. If the song has little or nothing to do with the rest of the service, it becomes just something extra that is thrown in, rather than an integral component to the worship experience.

Stories and Mini-Sermons

Stories are often at the heart of worship services designed for children. Catherine Stonehouse, in *Joining Children on the Spiritual Journey: Nurturing a Life of Faith*, explains that because children process deep realities before they can conceptualize them, stories can be an effective tool to help them mull over these ideas at an affective level. She says that in order for us "to give the great realities of faith to children, those realities must be in story form."

Selecting Stories

Not all stories are appropriate for a worship service. Ideally, a good story complements the worship theme for the day and communicates a value or idea about what it means to be a Unitarian Universalist.

Stories from many religious traditions can be a good source of wisdom and knowledge. Also, many folktales teach important lessons about how to live, the value of sharing with others, living together in peace, and the importance of taking care of the earth. These are all excellent concepts to build worship around.

A good story has a well-developed plot, distinct characters, and a clear problem to be solved. The resolution to the problem comes after some initial difficulty. Then, at the climax, the issue is resolved (either satisfactorily or not so satisfactorily) and a lesson about life is communicated.

Many children's books have simple plots, memorable characters, and easily understood lessons. These lend themselves well to use in worship with children, and many have pictures that add to the experience of sharing the story. For example, *The Lorax* by Dr. Seuss stresses the importance of taking care of our natural resources, *Old Turtle* by Douglas Wood reveals ideas about the nature of God, and *Giraffes Can't Dance* by Giles Andreae communicates the importance of individuality and uniqueness.

Worship leaders can also get books containing a number of stories within one volume. The stories are often grouped around a central theme or idea and can be used in multiple services. Books such as *Earth Tales From Around the World* by Michael Caduto, *Peace Tales* by Margaret Read MacDonald, and *Ready-To-Tell Tales* by David Holt and Bill Mooney all offer a number of stories appropriate for children's worship services. (For more titles of children's books to use as part of a worship service, see Storybooks, page 222.)

When selecting a book for use in worship with children, consider not only how an adult might interpret the story but also how children might view the events it describes. According to psychologist Jean Piaget in *The Psychology of the Child*, young children do not think the way adults do; they rely on intuition rather than logic. As a result, the connections children make with a story may differ from those adults make, and some stories may have an effect quite different from what was intended. Carolyn Brown, in *You Can Preach to the Kids, Too: Designing Sermons for Children and Adults*, reports that while some stories in the Bible may have spiritual meaning for adults, children may be terrified by them. Being sensitive to these differences in perception can help guide the selection of stories.

Telling vs. Reading

Using stories effectively in worship services does not mean simply finding a book and reading it word for word from beginning to end. Good stories in worship are told rather than read to the participants. Maintaining eye contact is important to sustaining listeners' interest during the telling of the story.

Good storytellers pause frequently to set the tone, create suspense, and let the participants absorb the crucial elements of the story. They also vary the volume and intensity of their voices to emphasize important points or establish a mood. Sounding frightened, angry, or happy (when the events in the story warrant such emotion) adds important color to a story. However, use caution when trying different accents or voices; the result could produce laughter that might distract listeners from the true meaning of the story. There is also the danger that using different voices or accents might come off as mocking or insulting to the groups of people who are imitated.

For worship leaders who are uncomfortable with telling the story, there are some ways to improve a presentation even while reading. Practicing reading the story aloud several times can improve the flow of the words; it also provides the opportunity to read it different ways to see which is most effective. Rehearsal has the added benefit of making it easier to look away from the page regularly and then find the place in the story again. If a leader is familiar enough with the story to make eye contact and simply glance at the page at regular intervals, it will help create the impression that the leader is telling the story rather than reading the words.

Another method is to use a finger to keep track of the right place in the story, allowing the storyteller to easily glance down when necessary. Reading the story word for word is usually not crucial; communicating the general concept is the key to effective storytelling, not reciting the actual words themselves. So it's best to simply continue reading if an error occurs. Chances are, the listeners will not even know that the wrong word was used or a particular phrase was left out.

Skilled readers are comfortable holding a picture book off to the side so it is visible to listeners. Familiarity with the story line and wording helps the reader merely glance sideways at the book for reminders as the story proceeds.

Rev. Carol Taylor uses an innovative technique to hold a book up for a group as she reads it. She writes the words of the story on paper or Post-it notes and sticks them to the back of the book. Then she can read the story word for word while holding the book up to let listeners see the pictures.

Experimenting with different methods can help storytellers determine the approach that is most comfortable for them.

Interactive Storytelling

The shorter the better is a useful principle in selecting stories for children's worship, particularly when young children will be present. Listeners' attention may wander if the story takes too long to get to the point. If the children do not pay attention, it does not matter how good the story is.

However, it is possible to use longer stories and keep the attention of even very young children by using a few innovative techniques. Encouraging children to act out portions of the story, make hand motions or sounds as part of the action unfolds, and repeat a line that occurs multiple times are all good ways to use longer, more involved stories with positive results.

For example, when using the story *We're Going on a Bear Hunt* by Michael Rosen and Helen Oxenbury, children can act out the story by slapping their hands on their thighs and clapping their hands at appropriate moments in the story. Children can be encouraged to make animal noises to correspond with the characters in the classic folktale "The Little Red Hen" or join in saying the line "Not I!," which occurs over and over again in the story.

Longer stories can also be accompanied by props, such as a kettle with a rock and assorted vegetables for the folktale "Stone Soup" or paper hearts for the story *What Is Love?* by Etan Boritzer. Other props that might be used to illustrate themes are autumn leaves (transitions or change), feathers (flight or sky), and yarn (the web of life).

Even the simple use of questions throughout the reading can help sustain interest during a long story. The worship leader can pause every now and then to ask listeners a question, such as "What do you think is going to happen next?" or "Is that a good idea?" Storytellers should be prepared for some wild and way-out answers as well as some very thoughtful ones and should be ready to bring the group back to the story if some of those answers threaten to pull the service too far off track.

Generally, when interactive elements are incorporated into a story, more interest will be sustained and more children will enjoy the experience. Participants cannot "get it" if they don't pay attention to the story.

Multi-Sensory Storytelling

A good story uses more than just the sense of hearing to involve participants. Visual elements in the form of pictures or props help generate and hold interest as the story is told or read to the group. However, there is no reason to feel limited to only the visual and auditory senses when using stories as part of worship.

The smell or even taste of homemade bread can complement a story about bread or coming home. Candles as part of a winter service can add a beautiful and powerful element, particularly if scented candles are used to evoke memories of family traditions around the holidays. Special food is essential for any sort of Seder service and can also be used in celebrating other special holidays, such as Divali or Day of the Dead.

To incorporate the sense of touch, shells or smooth stones can be passed among the participants during a story about the sea or other body of water. Children can plant flowers or vegetables as part of a service celebrating the arrival of spring or focusing on the importance of taking care of our earth.

By going beyond simply telling the tale, worship leaders can present a highly memorable experience. The lesson behind the story is synthesized and processed by individuals on a deeper level when multiple senses are involved and different learning styles are considered. Through a little creativity and imagination, the story becomes more than words; it is absorbed and an "Aha!" moment is created for the participants, who may then come away from the worship transformed by the experience.

Mini-Sermons

When sermons are used as part of children's worship, they may be referred to as mini-sermons because they are much shorter than traditional sermons and usually involve interaction with the participants. Questions may be asked and ideas may be solicited as part of the mini-sermon. A prop or visual may be associated with the idea behind the mini-sermon, such as an umbrella to symbolize the church community or a box of crayons to represent diversity.

Mini-sermons are addressed directly to the participants to draw them into the service, and unlike most stories, they state clearly the lesson to be learned. They do not have characters who think and act as part of the overall lesson. However, just like good stories, mini-sermons teach important lessons and are designed to appeal to children. Both stories and mini-sermons rely on well-crafted messages and well-executed presentations.

Themes of mini-sermons often center around what it means to be a Unitarian Universalist, explain a concept behind one of the seven Principles, or explore aspects of the six Sources of our living tradition. These short sermons are an effective way to communicate important ideas and moral ways of living as part of a worship service for children.

Meditation and Prayer

The spiritual practices of meditation and prayer promote emotional healing and a deeper awareness of both the self and the world. John Hudson, in *Instant Meditation for Stress Relief*, says that although meditation is associated primarily with the religious traditions of Buddhism and Hinduism, some form of the practice is used in most major religions of the world. Many Unitarian Universalists find it an enriching experience that promotes spiritual awareness and self-discovery.

In addition to its use as a personal spiritual practice, meditation is frequently an integral part of Unitarian Universalist worship services. It can be spoken, guided, or silent, depending on the framework of the service.

Meditation and prayer in children's worship calms the children's bodies and minds. More than a temporary method to induce relaxation, regular meditation teaches children a useful technique that they can rely on to help them in difficult times. Meditation can also serve as a form of prayer or reflection. As children grow older, they can use meditation to engage in positive self-talk or focus their thoughts during times of stress.

No technique can more effectively help Unitarian Universalist children deal with the transitions and challenges they will face in life. Knowing how to use meditation is a valuable skill that promotes the kind of soul-searching necessary to guide a person through times of uncertainty or to keep one calm during times of stress. Furthermore, no other spiritual practice is as compatible with the diverse theologies of Unitarian Universalism as meditation. Meditation is a tool for self-discovery and self-expression, but can also be a way to move beyond the ordinariness of life into the greater mystery.

For those children and families who find prayer meaningful, offering opportunities to explore the words and ways of praying as a Unitarian Universalist is invaluable. Through prayer children can learn to express gratitude and celebrate the specialness of life.

Religious Traditions

As a spiritual practice, meditation is most closely associated with the religious traditions of Hinduism and Buddhism and was the main vehicle through which Siddhartha Gautama (the Buddha) finally attained enlightenment. Buddhist thought encourages many stages of meditation, which are practiced in order to purify the mind, clear away distracting thoughts, and live in the present in order to more fully experience the world.

Yoga, one of the best-known practices of meditation, engages both the body and the mind in spiritual centering. Hatha yoga involves a series of physical exercises or postures designed to improve physical as well as mental control. Both this type of meditation, associated with the traditional religious practice of Hinduism, and Tai Chi from the Taoist tradition have become popular ways to reduce stress and promote relaxation through mental centering exercises paired with physical movements.

Hudson points out that in Christian religious communities such as convents and monasteries, monks, nuns, and priests may spend a period of time each day in quiet contemplation, often focusing upon a crucifix or rosary. In fact, the rosary that Catholics use to guide them through prayer serves as a meditative practice in that it involves a series of repetitive words. The prayers follow a specific order, much like a meditative mantra, while fingers hold the beads of the rosary. Both the prayer beads used by some Buddhists and the Catholic rosary serve to focus the mind on the rhythm of the prayers. The uniform size of the beads, their gentle, round shape and smooth surfaces, and the sound of their rhythmic clicking as they are pressed against one another assist in achieving the necessary centering for meditation.

The body prayers practiced by Muslims are also meditative, involving repeated movements and words. Through engaging in these repetitive acts, the body relaxes and the mind gets more centered. This focusing of the mind and body promotes a deeper emotional state and clearer spiritual awareness.

Effective Meditation Techniques

The most important part of effective meditation is obtaining a relaxed or deeply focused state. Regulating breathing and focusing on that breathing is not only physically calming, it also promotes concentration as the mind is cleared of intrusive thoughts. Cleansing breaths are taken in through the nostrils to fully expand the lungs and then are exhaled through the lips.

As with other elements in children's worship, the use of meditation must be consistent for greatest effect. Setting the tone with an opening ritual establishes the right mood and prepares children for the experience. An introduction to the meditation practice can be auditory (a bell or chime) or verbal (such as, "Now it's time to quiet our bodies and our minds through meditation").

Involving several senses in the meditation helps draw children deeper into the experience. Leaders often use a repetitive sound, or mantra, to clear the mind of distractions. The constant repetition of a phrase, word, or particular sound ("Om" or "aum" is frequently used by practitioners of Hinduism), along with the natural rhythm of breathing, enhances the meditative state. This mantra need not be a special word, chant, or incantation; some people find that simply repeating the words "relax" or "breathe" is highly effective.

Other sounds that can be used to focus the mind are the natural sounds of running water, ocean waves, rustling leaves, a steady drumbeat, or the sounds of a forest. Many meditative CDs are available that incorporate natural sounds with soft, soothing music.

Colors or special objects can also help focus attention during meditation. Children who are comfortable closing their eyes can visualize a color or a shape in their minds. Alternatively, the worship leader can encourage children to keep their eyes focused on an object placed on a worship table or hanging on the wall.

People have long used the sense of touch to induce a state of meditation and focus the mind. Participants can rub beads or smooth stones in the palms of their hands as they concentrate on the texture and shape.

Some congregations use burning incense or aromatic candles as part of meditation in worship services. While this can be an effective way of engaging additional senses in the process, it's important to make sure that no one who will participate in the worship service has a sensitivity to such smells. For some people, scents carry memories and feelings as well as the possibility of allergic reactions. Even if the worship leader is sure that none of the participants is overly sensitive to fragrances and perfumes, the possibility that a new child might arrive who is allergic is perhaps a reason not to include this element in children's worship services at all.

Spoken Meditations

There are two types of spoken meditations that may be used in worship: those in which participants speak together and those in which participants listen. While both of these meditation techniques are effective elements for children's worship services, the method that invites children to speak the meditation can facilitate the retention of the words and the ideas behind them when the service is over. Like responsive readings, meditations that require children to speak the words should be used judiciously so the needs of children who struggle with reading are taken into account. This challenge can be overcome by using the same meditation words for each service or by using a short meditation that can be spoken first by the worship leader and then by the participants. Longer meditations can be presented in call-back fashion, with the worship leader speaking one line at a time and then encouraging the participants to repeat the line before moving on to the next sentence.

Guided Meditations

Individuals or groups often use guided meditations through a process of relaxation and visualization. The words, spoken in a slow, soft, rhythmic manner, help to focus the brain not only on the spoken words but also on the visuals they evoke. Images and multi-sensory explorations are encouraged through the guidance of the worship leader's words.

Participants are invited to close their eyes during guided meditations in order to achieve optimum results. Relaxation is very important for deep processing of visualizations, and most guided meditations start with directions for relaxation and breathing. Pauses and lengthy silences are an essential part of this type of meditation, particularly if the leader asks questions that participants must consider and then either visualize or answer for themselves.

The pauses may seem unnaturally long to the person speaking the guided meditation; however, with practice it becomes easier to gauge the right length. Because these pauses are such a crucial part of guided meditations, some worship leaders count silently in order to ensure that enough time has passed before moving on to the next words. Other worship leaders extend pauses by silently forming their own answers or developing the ideas within their own minds. Practicing by recording the spoken meditation and then playing it back gives an idea of the listeners' perspective and a way to judge whether the pauses are long enough.

Because guided meditations involve visualizations and deep processing of inner thoughts, the end of the process must be intentionally delicate. Abruptly ending any kind of meditative experience can be jarring, and even more so for guided meditation. Increasing the length of the pauses as the meditation comes to an end is one way to help ease the transition. Leaders can conclude with an invitation like "Join us when you feel ready" or "When you are able, come back to this room," even if such direction is not built into the writing of the guided meditation.

A final pause, allowing participants to ease themselves through the transition, is a good way to complete the process. Or, end the guided meditations with a brief silent meditation and close with an auditory cue such as a gong, bell, or chime.

Walking Meditations

Buddhist monks have been known to walk up and down the same path in the forest day after day, moving very slowly as they concentrate on the movement of their feet, the changing pressure on the soles of their feet, and the feel of the ground as they step. The rhythm of the steps and the repetitive movement serve as a focusing center for the mind so that it may be emptied of other thoughts. Walking meditations and their physical movement serve the same function as regulating breathing or rubbing beads between the fingers.

Walking meditations are good to use with a large group of children who have trouble sitting quietly. This type of meditation can teach mind-focusing and the skill of being present in the moment without the requirement to sit still and relax. The practice of walking while meditating helps fill children's need for physical movement and allows them to concentrate on the rhythm of that movement.

Using a steady drumbeat or a simple chant to which children are encouraged to match their steps can strengthen the experience and help them focus on the movement. The drum or vocalization keeps their attention on the walking and helps keep the movement at a steady pace. It also helps reduce the possibility of distraction and the children's urge to talk to one another.

Music Meditations

Musical accompaniment can deepen the meditative experience, no matter the type of meditation. A steady drumbeat or a rhythmic chime or gong helps to focus the mind while being present in the moment. Repetitive words used as a chant can also have the same effect, whether they are spoken by those meditating or not.

Sometimes music itself is the focusing agent of the meditation. A light and airy flute or reverent violin selection performed live or on a CD can serve this function. Participants can create their own visualizations or simply be present and allow themselves to be absorbed in the music.

Brief music meditations can also be used as an effective transition from other types of meditation. Music provides a peaceful way to move beyond the earlier meditation into another state conducive to the next element of worship.

Using Prayer with Children

While some Unitarian Universalists consider meditation a substitute for prayer, for others prayer is an essential spiritual practice. Spoken prayers that are used repeatedly can even serve a meditative function as the familiar words focus the mind. This practice can promote deeper spiritual awareness and a sense of connection to others.

Prayer can be an essential part of children's worship, partly for the meditative effects it produces and partly for the spiritual practice of prayer itself. Using the same prayer for each worship and pairing it with hand or body motions serves as a defining ritual and a way to celebrate life or the divine.

When using prayer with children, it is important to be selective. Just as songs with words beyond their vocabulary will pass right over their heads, prayers with words beyond their understanding will also be ineffective. The younger the child, the simpler the words should be.

One way to think of prayer is to distinguish four basic types: praise, thanksgiving, petition, and contrition. Perhaps the most common and familiar of these types is petition. Many of the prayers found in the Hebrew Bible are prayers of petition in which people directly ask a higher power to fulfill their needs. Other prayers involve confessing wrongdoing, expressing contrition, and asking for forgiveness.

For children, prayers of thanksgiving and praise can be valuable exercises for appreciating the world we live in. For Unitarian Universalists who believe in a divine presence, such prayers can allow them to express deep feelings of reverence. Unitarian Universalists who do not hold a belief in a higher power can use these types of prayers to express appreciation for everyday events and to recognize the specialness of life.

An effective approach with older children is to choose diverse prayers from a variety of religious traditions. Prayers from different faiths expose children to the wisdom of many religions of the world. However, when using prayers from specific religious traditions, it is important to keep in mind what is appropriate to "borrow" and what might be considered cultural misappropriation. (For more on this idea, see Holidays and Cultural Misappropriation on page 84.)

No matter what technique you choose, meditation and prayer are spiritual practices that help people develop an inner sense of peace and self-awareness. More than relaxing both mind and body, they are meant to encourage people to concentrate on the here and now, to be "in the moment," and to be in touch with their inner calm. Chogyam Trungpa, in *The Path Is the Goal: A Basic Handbook of Buddhist Meditation,* says that prayer can help people unmask themselves as well as bring out the subtleties of intelligence inherent in all of us. It can be a way to realize the basic truths of life so that we can work on our own spiritual growth.

In the article "Meditation with Children: A Guide" on the UUA website, religious educator Susan Freudenthal asserts that "to hold a sacred moment within and sometimes to let it sail forth is a gift we can give to our children and youth. It can have meaning . . . when made relevant and when practiced consistently." She believes that in a world in which so many children are over-programmed with playgroups, school, athletics, and other activities, meditation can serve as a spiritual tool to help them slow down and appreciate the here and now amidst the stimulation all around them.

However, for children to truly experience the life-changing benefits of meditation or prayer, it must be done consistently. According to Freudenthal, meditation "should be included in children's, intergenerational, and youth worship either weekly or bi-weekly." Using the same type of meditation or prayer for each worship service is also important. While it is valuable for children to discover a multitude of ways in which a person can meditate or pray, it takes time and repeated experience for a child to understand a practice well enough to incorporate it personally.

Freudenthal also contends that "knowing how to be mindful of one's physical being, finding the space within to truly listen to your heart's songs, listening to your breath, and slowing down just for a few moments are priceless tools for young and old alike." Perhaps through meditation or prayer, our children can learn to be not just seekers but finders.

Themes

Preparing for quality children's worship services involves a sequence of steps, covered by the earlier chapters in this book. First, goals for the worship are established, then styles of worship are developed. Leaders then decide who the worship is for—children of all ages, elementary-age children only, or children along with their parents or guardians. Next, leaders create a framework for the service, with an orderly flow of events to move through the experience in a logical order, before they select the elements that make up the content of the service, such as songs, meditations, prayers, litanies, and mini-sermons. Now all that is needed is something to pull it all together—a theme.

A theme serves as an umbrella, joining together all the disparate elements that have been selected as content. It is *what the service is about* on that particular day.

While the framework and certain elements remain consistent from service to service, a theme allows the leader to add some variety to the worship. For services that contain relatively similar elements every week, a theme may be simply a topic for the story or mini-sermon. However, in services where the readings and songs change from time to time, the theme can be woven throughout. Songs, responsive readings, litanies, and prayers all can be chosen based on the theme of that day's worship.

Holidays and Cultural Misappropriation

Building services around holidays and other special events provides common themes for worship. People feel the need to celebrate holidays, and worship services are a great way to meet this need. Sometimes there is lower attendance at church services on minor holidays, so finding a unique way to present holiday programs can boost attendance or fill a special need for those who do attend.

Celebrating holidays and the holy days of many faiths can help children to have fun as they learn about the beliefs of other religions. However, as Unitarian Universalists we must be careful not to engage in cultural misappropriation. Without a proper context, adopting the rituals and practices of other cultures and faiths can demean the practices rather than affirm them.

Jacqui James, the former anti-oppression programs and resources director for the Religious Education Department of the Unitarian Universalist Association, has written on this topic in her online article "Reckless Borrowing or Appropriate Cultural Sharing?" She says it is important to "think about honoring differences versus appropriating them." James maintains that Unitarian Universalists should consider their actions each time they use the spiritual symbols, artifacts, and symbols of another faith tradition.

Any creation of worship using ritual and spirituality from other cultures can raise concern about whether it is possible to authentically incorporate these elements. James writes, "With our ready access to information, it is easy to find books, music, meditation, and rituals from around the world. However, making sense of these traditions and integrating them coherently is not as easy. There is a real danger of misrepresenting and misunderstanding another tradition."

James notes that while there is no one answer to dealing with issues of cultural misappropriation, as Unitarian Universalists committed to a responsible search for truth and meaning, it is imperative for us to consider the matter and act accordingly. The challenge of appropriate cultural sharing relates to the borrower's motivation and the context. Without proper context, adopting others' rituals and spiritual practices is degrading, not celebratory. If the borrowed element is distorted, watered down, or misrepresented, then its use is improper.

Worship with holiday themes should positively reinforce the cultures that originated the holidays. Affirming that these practices belong to another faith tradition is an important step toward offering respect rather than ridicule.

Principles and Sources

Themes for children's worship can help build a sense of what it means to be a Unitarian Universalist. Some services focus on one of the seven Principles, even if a regular part of the framework includes a ritual on all seven Principles. Themes incorporating one of the Principles can include a story or mini-sermon on the Principle of the Day, and the selection of songs, readings, and other elements of the service can complement this focus (if such elements change on a regular basis).

Exploring any one of the six Sources of our living tradition or the concept of the Sources in their entirety can also be effective themes for helping children understand their religious tradition. Due to the richness of material contained in the Sources, some congregations have spent an entire year on various themes relating to these ideas.

Matching Learning Experiences

Children's worship can also be designed to complement or supplement the educational theme that is addressed by the curriculum that RE teachers are following. The weekly or monthly children's worship then enriches the learning experience in the classroom, allowing children to explore similar themes through both worship and curriculum.

Using themes related to world religions, a different religious tradition can be explored in each worship service. One week, children's worship might use a story and meditation based on the Buddhist tradition, while the next week it could celebrate the arrival of spring in the pagan tradition.

Some congregations pick worship themes that are intentionally different from the current curriculum. For instance, the worship could focus on world religions while children concentrate on UU identity through curriculum instruction or workshops. This allows children to be exposed to two different concepts in a given year.

Some congregations try to match their theme for children's worship to the theme of the main worship service. This is a good way to link the two services, particularly if children first spend time in the main service and then leave to attend a service designed for them. It is also an excellent way to unify the experiences for families whose members are worshiping in separate spaces. Families can talk about their worship services when they are together again, and parents are aware of what children explored because it was similar to their own experience.

However, this can be tricky to pull off in practice, because many themes of adult worship are not easily translated into terms children can understand. Also, children need a strong sense of what their religion means to them and how to live their lives as Unitarian Universalists. They need to know why their religion is important and relevant. They have not rejected any concepts or decided on their preferences because they are still learning what it all means. Adults, on the other hand, may believe that they already understand Unitarian Universalist values and may not prefer worship themes about these basics of their faith.

Different Life Experiences

When planning themes for worship, it is important to consider the different life experiences of the children. Even those of similar age have had a wide variety of experiences. For example, themes about family should acknowledge diversity, because not every child is raised in a two-parent home by a mother and a father.

Children who have a parent who is not Unitarian Universalist may be learning another faith tradition as well as Unitarian Universalism; for these children, any references to their "other" religion may bring up concerns or issues that wouldn't necessarily occur to another child.

Celebrating the Day of the Dead (a Mexican holiday honoring the spirits of loved ones who have died) is an example of a theme that should be approached with caution. The celebration comes from a particular cultural tradition, so leaders should be sure to set it in proper context (to learn more about cultural holidays see Multicultural Resources, page 245). Also, children's experiences with death vary considerably. While most children will share about a pet dying, others may be struggling with the recent loss of a grandparent, sibling, or parent. For them, such a theme will have a much different meaning, and their reactions are likely to be very different as well.

Recognizing such differences, leaders can present the theme in a sensitive way, taking into account the deep feelings aroused in some children during the service. Themes should be approached reverently, appreciating the variety of life experiences represented among the participants.

Relevance

Gail Forsyth-Vail, director of religious education at North Parish of North Andover, Massachusetts, creates her plan for worship a year in advance, developing themes based in part on holidays and special events at her congregation. She designs an overall plan with a message she thinks will resonate with the children and relate to their lives. Every theme she selects has to speak in some way to the children (and the adults in the case of intergenerational or multi-generational worship).

Whether using stories from the Bible, wisdom from the world's religions, segments of UU history, experiences in the natural world, or celebrations of holidays from other faith traditions, relevance is key to selecting a theme. Without relevance, the essential message of a worship service is lost. When children do not understand an idea because it is beyond their experience, a valuable opportunity for transformational worship is relinquished. Themes can be unique or traditional, but if they do not fit within a child's view of the world, they are ineffective.

Intergenerational Worship

Offering worship services aimed at the spiritual development of children invites our young ones to experience Unitarian Universalism in their own way and on their own terms. When worship services are designed to meet their needs, children can experience ritual, expand their faith development, connect with their peers, and understand the intimacy necessary to learn spiritual techniques such as meditation. Sophia Cavaletti, in *The Religious Potential of the Child*, writes that if children do not have a place where they can grasp the deep realities of faith in a way that is suitable to their youthful rhythm, they may pass through life without ever being able to internalize these realities.

However, children also need the opportunity to worship with the entire faith community. If they are shuttled away to their own worship service and religious education program separate from adults every Sunday morning, they will have little chance to feel like a true part of their religious community. In *Joining Children on the Spiritual Journey: Nurturing a Life of Faith*, Catherine Stonehouse maintains that participation in the life and events of the faith community as a whole is necessary for the healthy spiritual growth of children, and the most effective way to do this is for children and adults to worship together. Whether it is for fifteen minutes every Sunday or for the full service, having all ages worship together is good for the whole faith community.

Welcoming children into the primary worship service invites children into the heart of a congregation. According to Catherine

Stonehouse, "deep bonds often form between adults and children who experience worship together." She asserts that when "young and old in the community of faith . . . journey together in commitment to one another . . . (a) beautiful, enriching spiritual formation occurs for all. When children are included as respected, active participants in the community of faith, they draw us back into the story of our faith and help us reactivate our imaginations to experience the story anew."

However, merely having children present in the service is not enough to create an environment in which young and old can worship together. If children are to be present and actually gain something positive from the experience, Catherine Stonehouse says, the service should be planned with them in mind. A worship service that includes persons of all ages must be designed to accommodate the needs and interests of people in all life stages.

Forcing children to sit through a service aimed at adults so that they can "learn how worship happens" will backfire if children become bored, restless, or anxious. They may learn instead to seriously dislike going to church. When the church becomes a place of discomfort and unhappiness, then children will choose not to attend as soon as they are able. "I was a preacher's kid who had to attend church every time the doors were open and sit through long, boring services where people talked and talked and talked," explains Jolinda Stephens, director of lifespan religious programming at the Unitarian Universalist Church of the Monterey Peninsula in California. "I hated it. That's about all I learned—that I hated it."

After all, how many adults would continue to attend a worship service where they sat in chairs that were much too small? How many adults would enjoy and willingly return for a service spoken in an unfamiliar language? How many would choose to go to a service in which participants were forced to do calisthenics when they would prefer to just sit and relax?

This is in effect what we require of our children when we ask them to sit in chairs that are too large through a long service that uses too many unfamiliar words, appeals to a sophisticated intellect, and requires participants to sit still and listen when they would prefer to move. Not only are there many words that children don't understand, often the very concepts being discussed are beyond their understanding. Sermons in services aimed at adults frequently reference the concerns of adults (such as mortgages, car payments, and maintaining relationships). On the other hand, worship services that are designed for all ages include universal themes and elements through which multiple levels of meaning can be invoked. Such themes and elements can be explored in multiple ways to meet the needs of many different people who perceive things in diverse ways. A true intergenerational service is crafted to meet the needs of both the children and the adults who are present.

Layering and Weaving

It is not easy to structure a worship service that engages, challenges, and satisfies a wide array of ages, needs, and learning styles. Like worship services for a wide age span of children, multigenerational worship services include elements that are important for different stages of faith development. They may include movement and ritual for the preschoolers, stories of ethical choices for elementary-age children, and some moments of insight for adults.

Rev. Greg Ward, in the on-line article "Philosophy of Inter-generational Services," reports that the objective of such services "is not to cater to just one facet of a community but to maintain a responsible middle ground such that the vast majority will be asked to stretch without being dismissed." It is important to present information that is relevant to the children and their developmental level, but it is also important to provide opportunities for the older members of the congregation to wrestle with the ideas that are presented and to consider the relevance of these messages to their own lives.

Effective intergenerational services are structured with multiple levels, or layers, of meaning. Peeling such a service, like peeling away the layers of an onion, means coming closer to the strongest and most pungent part of it. While preschoolers may only be able to uncover the outside layer, elementary-age children can peel away a bit more, youth and adults yet more, with some adults able to reach the very core.

On the surface, the multigenerational worship service may be designed to follow the format and structure of a children's worship service (with many elements selected to appeal to their interests), but sprinkled throughout are little tidbits of deeper meaning for the adults to grasp. Worship services for persons of all ages can be developed using the concepts explored in earlier chapters of this book. Weaving these ideas together with some strands of wisdom and opportunities for deeper reflection for adults can create an enriching worship experience for all ages. Understanding what children need from worship, while keeping in mind the needs of adults, a worship leader can design a service to meet the needs of the entire congregation.

Stories as a Focus

Classic stories have a powerful ability to be engaging and thought-provoking on many different levels. Catherine Stonehouse explains that a primary characteristic of quality literature for children is a story that fascinates the child and yet provides insight and humor for the adult. *The Lorax* by Dr. Seuss is one example of a story with many elements that appeal to both children and adults, but on different levels. Children are engaged by the story and as a result are able to easily grasp the message about taking care of our environment; the message of renewal and hope at the end resonates with the older members of the congregation. This story can be the basis of a worship service for both young and old when used with complementary songs, meditations, and readings.

According to Ward, the objective is to offer "more grist for the mental mill that older members need while not belaboring the intellectual/conceptual side and extending beyond the bounds of the younger attention span." Using a classic story as a focus, and then adding more meaning for the adults through careful selection of hymns, readings, and litanies is an optimum way to offer multi-generational worship.

Beyond the Words

Since many elders also struggle with reading (for different reasons, such as failing eyesight), using elements that do not require reading can actually accommodate the needs of both the youngest and oldest members of the congregation at the same time. In place of responsive readings that require reading ability, litanies can engage participants on multiple levels. The response line that the congregation repeats helps to reinforce the basic message with children, and the verses between the repetitions can be a conduit for providing greater depth of insight for older persons. Alternately, responsive readings can be shared as a call-back, with the participants in worship "calling back" the words just spoken by the worship leader.

While it is not necessary to include only songs with words that are understood by preschool children, it is important to remember that if there are too many words that are not understood, children will begin to tune out. According to Jolinda Stephens, multigenerational worship services should include music that appeals to everyone and "enough movement to help the kids and (even some) older adults . . . move around to cope with the hour."

Movement in the service can help meet the needs of those with short attention spans or those not accustomed to processing information orally. Inviting people to come forward to light a candle, drop a pebble in a bowl of water, or even pass a basket of shells around the room are simple ways to incorporate movement. Prayers or songs that have hand or body motions are also great ways to add movement to a service. If children regularly use a prayer, special song, or ritual in their children's worship, they can come forward to lead the congregation in performing it.

Building a service around numerous shorter elements rather than leading up to a long sermon can also help meet the challenge posed by short attention spans. If a longer sermon or story is necessary, it can be divided into two or three shorter segments separated by other, more engaging elements.

Since children are also highly visual, they are particularly sensitive to the environment in which worship takes place. They are more apt to pay attention to a story or sermon if visual representations are used to complement it, such as pictures displayed on a large screen or people up front acting out the story.

Using actual props can help illustrate a point in a concrete way for children who learn by doing rather than listening. The following example of an effective use of props comes from Linda Olson Peebles in the book about intergenerational worship, *Windmills, Worship and Wonder.* While a sermon can include an analogy for adults that compares spoken words with toothpaste squeezed from a tube, children are more likely to be engaged when asked to squeeze all of the toothpaste from a real tube and then, once it is all out, asked to put it back in. The realization that it is impossible to do so affects them on a level much deeper than if they had merely heard the analogy presented in a sermon. At the same time, the adults who witness the children's reactions when told to put the toothpaste back in the tube are able to process the experience on a different level. The abstraction is made real and the concept tangible when they experience it from the children's perspective. If this concept is reinforced by a subsequent reading on the importance of treating others fairly, the needs of adults hungry for insight are met and the children can also appreciate these words because they have already grasped and internalized the idea.

Keeping It Simple

Meditations in an intergenerational service should be brief because children will not cooperate with an extended period of centering if the words do not engage them. If children cannot cooperate with quiet minds and bodies during meditation, then the adults can't appreciate this time either. However, while selected meditations can be intentionally less abstract than those for a strictly adult service, they need not be solely on a preschooler's level. Many meditations and hymns are easily understood yet carry deep meaning and a potent message. Young children can also be engaged and quiet during a meaningful meditation for adults if they are given a special task as part of the process, such as ringing chimes at the end of each sentence or during pauses.

Many of the litanies and meditations in the resource section of this book can be used effectively with both children and adults. While the wording is relatively simple, the concepts expressed nevertheless resonate with adults. The meanings behind the words are universal, and therefore these elements can be effective with all ages. In fact, with this simpler format, some adults may even appreciate the chance to get a message delivered in a new way.

Rev. Tamara Lebak, who led multigenerational services at West Shore Church in Rocky River, Ohio, while she served as sabbatical minister, reported in a General Assembly presentation that when crafting worship services for all ages, it is important to keep the message clear. It may be tempting to use fancy words and a sophisticated vocabulary, but the same idea can usually be expressed with words that are simpler. She continually asked herself, "What is the ten-dollar word for what I'm trying to say? What do I want to say, and how can I say it so that it is relevant to everyone?"

Universal Themes

Finally, we all have a need to make sense of things, no matter what stage of life we are in. Including insights about topics such as a healthier way to approach conflict, how to work for justice in the world, or ways to appreciate the interdependent web is crucial to any intergenerational service. We come to a worship service not only to celebrate worth but to gain something worthy from the experience. In fact, the word worship is derived from "worthshipe," which can be translated to mean "worthiness." Therefore, when we worship, we celebrate that which we find most important.

Like the toothpaste analogy, such universal themes set the stage for an "Aha!" moment for children and adults alike. At one congregation, the toothpaste analogy was remembered and talked about for years after it was presented in worship. Parents used it to remind their children of the consequences of their actions, it was brought up at subsequent board meetings, and it was even employed at a rather contentious congregational meeting when tensions threatened to create an unhealthy atmosphere.

Intergenerational worship is important for any congregation. The children are able to connect to the faith life of the entire church community, participating in the most central aspect of its weekly rhythm. Adults, meanwhile, are led to greater spiritual insights by the presence of children in worship, benefiting from the distillation of complex ideas into simple but profound concepts.

Conclusion

Children possess an innate spirituality and deep sense of wonder about the world, but without guidance and the opportunity to celebrate the greater mystery, their faith development may never reach its full potential. As John J. Gleason notes in his book, *Growing Up to God: Eight Steps in Religious Development,* there are windows of opportunity for faith development to occur just as there are in other stages of human development. What children learn in their formative years can profoundly influence their future religious learning. If we neglect the spiritual formation of our children, we prevent the development of the very foundations of their faith.

Participating in the life of a religious community, while perhaps the most important element of a child's spiritual growth, is merely one component of what should be the overarching goal of faith development. Children need religious education and a sense of belonging to a beloved community, but they also need to express their spiritual natures through singing songs of celebration, expressing gratitude through prayers, or calming themselves through meditation. They need to hear stories that speak to their understandings, and they need to internalize the rituals that make their religion unique.

When we allow children to stretch themselves and encourage them to grow spiritually, we don't simply meet their needs; we find that we feed ourselves as well. Our own faith can be enriched by seeing the ordinary through their eyes and the seemingly simple things in life from an entirely new perspective.

Like *The Velveteen Rabbit*, who is made real by a child's love, we can allow children to guide us on a spiritual path with insights that are fresh and unique. We too are made "real" by the experience. Children easily express profound insights in simple ways, and they can break down complex ideas into amazing snippets. We may be their guides on their spiritual journeys, providing worship experiences that help develop their faith, but if we allow ourselves to go along, we can reach greater spiritual insights of our own.

Child-Friendly
Worship Resources

Collected here is an assortment of chalice lightings and opening words, meditations, prayers, responsive readings, stories, sermons, songs, and closing words that can be incorporated into a worship service for children. These child-friendly elements can be used in services for children of different ages or for children and their families worshiping together (see page 215 for sample services).

Many of these resources were graciously provided by my religious education colleagues in response to my request for resources to share. I have also included some poetry and prayers that embody the wisdom of several ancient cultures. I respectfully acknowledge the peoples who have created these and passed them from generation to generation. We cannot know how many people have shaped them over time. I urge you to teach the children something about the cultural context of an element whenever you use one from another culture. This is one way to affirm our Unitarian Universalist values of respect and inclusion. Some resources to help you learn more about the history and culture of other peoples are listed in the For More Information and Ideas section (page 221) along with suggestions about where you can find more worship materials for children.

Please note that certain elements—chalice lightings and opening words, spoken meditations, prayers, and closing words—are categorized according to the seven Unitarian Universalist Priniciples and the six Sources of our living tradition to help leaders find readings suited to certain key themes.

Chalice Lightings and Opening Words

We light this chalice
  [*make motion of striking match*]
to celebrate Unitarian Universalism.
  [*cup hands in shape of two Us*]
This is the church of the open mind,
  [*place hands over eyes and open like a door*]
the loving hearts,
  [*cross arms over chest*]
and the helping hands.
  [*hold hands out, palms up*]
We take care of the earth
  [*make circle with hands*]
and each other.
  [*spread out hands in inclusive gesture*]

—Anonymous

The flame rekindles;
our timeless chalice dances
with the light and warmth.

—Bryan Richards

We light this candle to remind ourselves
    to treat all people kindly.
We light this candle to remind ourselves
    to take good care of the earth.
We light this candle to remind ourselves
    to live lives full of goodness
    and love.

    —Anonymous

We gather here to worship:
    to seek the truth, to grow in love, to join in service;
    to celebrate life's beauty and find healing for its pain;
    to honor our kinship with each other and with the earth;
    to create a more compassionate world, beginning with ourselves;
    to wonder at the mystery that gave us birth;
    to find courage for the journey's end;
    and listen for the wisdom that guides us
        in the quiet of this moment.

    —Gary Kowalski

Life is a gift for which we are grateful.
We gather in community
to celebrate the glories and the mysteries
of this great gift.

    —Marjorie Montgomery

In the flame from this chalice
we find the light of faith,
the glow of hope,
and the warmth of service.
May we ever grow in faith, hope, and service
as we kindle our own lights from its spark.

—Anonymous

The inherent worth and dignity of every person

This is a community of compassion and welcoming.
You do not have to do anything to earn the love
    contained within these walls.
You do not have to be braver, smarter, stronger, better
than you are in this moment
    to belong here, with us.

—Erika Hewitt, adapted

This symbol of energy
of light, of life
to remind us
of the energy within us
of the light of our life
of the light that is in us
of the light that *is* us.

— Janet Goode

Justice, equity and compassion in human relations

May the light we now kindle
inspire us to use our powers
to heal and not to harm,
to help and not to hinder,
to bless and not to curse.

—Jewish proverb, adapted

To face the world's shadows,
   a chalice of light.
To face the world's coldness,
   a chalice of warmth.
To face the world's terrors,
   a chalice of courage.
To face the world's turmoil,
   a chalice of peace.
May its glow fill our spirits, our hearts,
   and our lives.

—Lindsay Bates

Acceptance of one another and encouragement to spiritual growth in our congregations

We light this chalice to rekindle
   our Flame of Truth.
We light this chalice to replenish
   our Spirit of Love.
We light this chalice to rededicate
   our Energy of Action.

—Makanah Morriss

To remember how we can live
To remember who we are
To create how we will be
We light this chalice.

—Barbara J. Pescan, adapted

Come into this circle of community. Come into this sacred space.
Bring your whole self!
Bring the joy that makes your heart sing.
Bring your kindness and your compassion.
Bring also your sadness and your disappointments.
Spirit of love and mystery, help us to recognize the spark of the divine
that lives inside each of us.
May we know the joy of being together.

—Andrew Pakula, adapted

A free and responsible search for truth and meaning

We light this chalice
in honor of the many changes in our lives.
We light this chalice
in honor of the growth in body and mind
and deepening of spirit and faith
we experience each day.

—Beth Casebolt, adapted

Chalice flame, burning bright,
symbol of my own light,
light around me, light aglow,
light that shines as I learn and grow,
light that shines as I learn and grow.

 —Beryl Aschenberg

Into this place may we come
 to share,
 to learn,
 to speak,
 to listen,
and to grow together in the spirit of peace and harmony
 and love.

 —Frances Reece Day

The right of conscience and the use of the democratic process

Come, let us worship together.
Let us open our minds to the challenge of reason,
 open our hearts to the healing of love,
 open our lives to the calling of conscience,
 open our souls to the comfort of joy.

Astonished by the miracle of life,
 grateful for the gift of fellowship,
 confident in the power of living faith,
  we are here gathered:

Come, let us worship together.

 —Lindsay Bates

Let us have faith that right makes might,
and in that faith, let us, to the end,
dare to do our duty as we understand it.

—Abraham Lincoln

World community, with peace, liberty and justice for all

Flaming chalice, burning bright,
now you share with us your light.
May we always learn to share
with all people, everywhere.

—Eva M. Češkava, adapted

Come into our circle of kindness
Come into our circle of peace
Come into our circle of friendship
Come be part of our circle of love

—Beth Casebolt

Respect for the interdependent web of all existence

We light this chalice
to celebrate the sun and stars
that float in the open air;
the apple-shaped Earth,
and we upon it.

—Walt Whitman, adapted

Water runs deep in the Earth.
Miraculously, water comes to us,
and sustains all life.

Water and sun
green these plants.
When the rain of compassion falls,
even a desert becomes an immense,
green ocean.

—Thich Nhat Hanh

This earthen chalice
was born of clay and water,
the flesh and blood of Gaia;
   Given form by the hand of the potter;
   Set by the bonding fire of the kiln.
As we touch the flame to her lips,
joining fire and air,
May her light remind us of that unity
      of earth, air, fire, and water,
      of plant and animal,
      human and mineral,
         that we and the earth are one.

—Edwin A. Lane

Direct experience of transcending mystery and wonder

We celebrate the mystery
We honor the wonder
We enjoy the magic of our world.

—Michelle Richards

We light this chalice
for the wonder everyone sees
in everyone else they see,
and the wonders that fill
each minute of time forever.

　　—Walt Whitman, adapted

Words and deeds of prophetic women and men

We light this chalice
in honor of the free mind—
the free mind with no boundaries
to its love.

　　—William Ellery Channing, adapted

Our Unitarian heritage bids us light our chalice
In the name of freedom,
In the light of reason,
In actions of tolerance.
We gather in community to celebrate a heritage of freedom, reason,
and tolerance.

Our Universalist heritage bids us light our chalice
In the name of faith,
In the light of hope,
In actions of love.

We gather in community to celebrate a heritage of faith, hope, and
love.

Let us bring this Unitarian Universalist heritage into our world and
our lives today.

　　—Elizabeth M. Strong

Wisdom from the world's religions

We bow unto the Light Divine that burns
Within every living soul.

   —Hindu chant

The light of this chalice reminds us
that it is a symbol
of all the world's religions.
This small light shines
as do the fires burned
to ward off the darkness
and welcome back the sun
in the Celtic and Native American faiths;
as do the Jewish Shabbat candles
and the Christian altar candles;
as do the oil lamps of the Hindu Divali
and the candles of Buddhism;
and it is a symbol of the light inside each of us, as recognized
    by Muslims;
it is a symbol of the sun
and evolution as studied by Humanists.
As we light this chalice,
may we be reminded that this light
is a symbol that ties us to many faiths,
beliefs, traditions, and customs
from which we can learn and enrich our lives.

   —Beth Casebolt

Jewish and Christian teachings

The wilderness and the dry land shall be glad,
    the desert shall rejoice and blossom;
like the crocus it shall blossom abundantly,
    and rejoice with joy and singing.

    —Isaiah 35:1-2

This is the day that the Lord has made;
    let us rejoice and be glad in it.

    —Psalm 118:24

Humanist teachings

We light this chalice
to celebrate our beginnings,
our cosmic origins
of dust and new stars,
of life that crawled from the sea
and walked upon land,
then harnessed the technology
to fly back up into the stars
from whence we came.

    —Michelle Richards

We light this chalice to remind us
in every speck of dust, in ourselves,
in visible and invisible worlds,
in planets, the sun and stars,

in joyous dance of atoms
is the laughter rippling through the universe.

   —Annie Dillard, adapted

Earth-centered traditions

There is only one great thing…
   the great day that dawns, and the light that fills the world.

   —Eskimo song

Light the sacred fire
In honor of the sacred one
Who teaches love, compassion, and honor
That we may heal the earth
And heal each other.

   —Ojibway

Spoken Meditations

UU Principles for Children

We believe

That each and every person is important

That all people should be treated fairly and kindly

That we should accept one another and keep on learning together

That each person must be free to search for what is true and right
in life

That all persons should have a vote about the things that concern
them

In working for a peaceful, fair, and free world

In caring for our planet earth, the home we share with all living
things.

—Ann Fields and Joan Goodwin

UU Sources for Children

We can look for answers
in the magic and mystery
in everything alive.

We can look for answers
in the words and deeds
of those men and women
who show us how to live fairly and in peace.

We can look for answers
in the sacred texts
and wisdom from the world's religions
which inspire us to do what's right.

We can look for answers
in Jewish and Christian teachings
which show us how to love our neighbor
and treat them how we wish to be treated.

We can look for answers
in reason and science
which help us to remember
just what is important
and what our choices mean.

We can look for answers
in religions which celebrate the earth
and show us how to live
in harmony with nature.

    —Michelle Richards

The inherent worth and dignity of every person

It's ok to cry, it's ok to be afraid, it's ok to be weak,
it's ok to be vulnerable, it's ok to be human.
It's from all these elements that we grow.

    —Kevin Morais

Sitting on the ground,
with the huge universe of sky
and space all around,
may we let our eyes be open
to the miracle of life
in every person whom we see.
May our hearts and minds
not be numb or unaware or unconcerned.
The vibrancy of life is all around.
The power of love and nurture
is ours to bring into being,
to help ourselves and every child we meet.
Who we are and how we are with one another matters.
May we bring blessing
and witness to the sacredness
of our being human.

—Linda Olson Peebles

Justice, equity and compassion in human relations

Never does hatred cease
by hating in return;
Only through love
can hatred come to an end.
Victory breeds hatred;
The conquered dwell in sorrow
and resentment.
They who give up all thought of victory
or defeat,
May *they* be calm
and live happily at peace.

—*Dhammapada*

What actions are most excellent?
To gladden the heart of a human being,
to feed the hungry, to help the afflicted,
to lighten the sorrow of the sorrowful and
to remove the wrongs of the injured.

   —The Prophet Muhammad (Peace Be Upon Him)

Acceptance of one another and encouragement to spiritual growth in our congregations

I am Unitarian,
I live and work in this faith.
Jesus is my guide
And God is my help.
We, humans, are all brothers and sisters,
Our law is one: love.
The goal of our work is shared,
Happy are those of God's Kingdom.

   —Transylvanian Blessing

May I know the circle of love
into which I was born.
May my life make the circle
wider and wider,
starting with my family and these friends,
starting today.

   —Betsy Darr

A free and responsible search for truth and meaning

Stay on the path if you're suffering
by taking the steps you need to take.
Hang on and hang in there, because it's now
that you're growing at light speed.
You're never going backward, only forward.

   —Kevin Morais

Finish every day and be done with it.
You have done what you could.
Some mistakes were made, for sure.
Forget them as soon as you can,
tomorrow is a new day;
begin it well and serenely,
with too high a spirit
to be burdened with your old nonsense.
This new day is too dear,
with its hopes and invitations,
to waste a moment on the yesterdays.

   —Ralph Waldo Emerson, adapted

The right of conscience and the use of the democratic process

May we find within ourselves
   the courage to be who we are.
May we know when it is time to listen
   and when it is time to speak.
May we trust ourselves to be the ones
   to find the words that need to be said
   or to do what needs to be done.

May we trust one another
   and know there are many ways
   to go through life.
May we know that though we cannot change some of what life
   gives to us,
we can choose how we deal with what we are given.

   —Barbara Hamilton Holway

Wouldn't it be great if we walked around
surrounded by our souls,
so that they were the first things people saw
instead of the last things?
Then people would judge us by who we really are
instead of how we look.
There would be no more thinking certain things about people
   because of the color of their skin or how tall they are
   or how much they weigh or how old they are.
Then people would work at making their souls more attractive
instead of their bodies and faces.

Imagine people knowing by your soul that you really need a hug.
Imagine people helping each other and their souls changing colors
   or even glowing.

   —Tess Baumberger, adapted

World community, with peace, liberty and justice for all

Better
than if there were thousands
of meaningless words is
one
meaningful

word
that on hearing
brings peace.

Better
than if there were thousands
of meaningless verses is
one
meaningful
verse
that on hearing
brings peace.

And better than chanting hundreds
of meaningless verses is
one
Dhamma-saying
that on hearing
brings peace.

—*Dhammapada*, translated by Thanissaro Bhikkhu

I will be truthful.
I will suffer no injustice.
I will be free from fear.
I will not use force.
I will be of good will to all.

—Mahatma Gandhi, adapted

Respect for the interdependent web of all existence

We give thanks for the earth and its creatures, and are grateful
    from A to Z:
For alligators, apricots, acorns, and apple trees,
For bumblebees, bananas, blueberries, and beagles,
Coconuts, crawdads, cornfields, and coffee,
Daisies, elephants, and flying fish,
For groundhogs, glaciers, and grasslands,
Hippos and hazelnuts, icicles and iguanas,
For juniper, jackrabbits, and junebugs,
Kudzu and kangaroos, lightning bugs and licorice,
For mountains and milkweed and mistletoe,
Narwhals and nasturtiums, otters and ocelots,
For peonies, persimmons, and polar bears,
Quahogs and Queen Anne's lace,
For raspberries and roses,
Salmon and sassafras, tornadoes and tulipwood,
Urchins and valleys and waterfalls,
For X (the unknown, the mystery of it all!)
In every yak and yam;
We are grateful, good Earth, not least of all,
For zinnias, zucchini, and zebras,
And for the alphabet of wonderful things
That are simple as ABC.

    —Gary Kowalski

Clouds are flowing in the river, waves are flying in the sky.
Life is laughing in a pebble. Does a pebble ever die?

Flowers grow out of the garbage, such a miracle to see.
What seems dead and what seems dying makes for butterflies
    to be.

Life is laughing in a pebble, flowers bathe in morning dew.
Dust is dancing in my footsteps and I wonder who is who.

Clouds are flowing in the river, clouds are drifting in my tea,
On a never-ending journey, what a miracle to be!

—Eveline Beumkes

Direct experience of transcending mystery and wonder

This life, you must know
as the tiny splash of a raindrop.

A thing of beauty that disappears as it comes into being.

Therefore, set your goal.
Make use of every day and every night.

—Je Tsongkhapa

Blessed by the Lord be the land,
with the precious gifts of heaven,
with the dew,
and the deep that lies beneath,
with the precious fruits
brought forth by the sun
and the riches brought forth by the moon,
with the greatness of the ancient mountains,
with the abundance of the everlasting hills,
and with all the treasures of the earth
in its perfection.

—Deuteronomy 33:13-16, adapted

Words and deeds of prophetic women and men

In a house which becomes a home, one hands down and another takes up the heritage of mind and heart, laughter and tears, musings and deeds.

—Antoine de St. Exupéry

People say,
"What is the sense of our small effort?"
They cannot see that
we must lay one brick at a time,
take one step at a time.
A pebble cast into a pond causes ripples
that spread in all directions.
Each one of our thoughts,
words and deeds is like that.
No one has a right to sit down
and feel hopeless.
There's too much work to do.

—Dorothy Day, adapted

Wisdom from the world's religions

To worship God is nothing other than to serve the people.
It does not need rosaries, prayer carpets, or robes.
All peoples are members of the same body, created from one essence.
If fate brings suffering to one member
the others cannot stay at rest.

—Saadi

This ritual is One.
The food is One.
We who offer the food are One.
The fire of hunger is also One.
All action is One.
We who understand this are One.

   —Hindu blessing

Jewish and Christian teachings

Ask, and it will be given you; search, and you will find; knock, and the door will be opened for you. For everyone who asks receives, and everyone who searches finds, and for everyone who knocks, the door will be opened.

   —Matthew 7:7-8

The good person out of the good treasure of the heart produces good, and the evil person out of evil treasure produces evil; for it is out of the abundance of the heart that the mouth speaks.

   —Luke 6:45

For everything there is a season,
and a time for every matter under heaven:
a time to be born, and a time to die;
a time to plant, and a time to pluck up what is planted;
a time to kill, and a time to heal;
a time to break down, and a time to build up;
a time to weep, and a time to laugh;
a time to mourn, and a time to dance;
a time to throw away stones, and a time to gather stones together;
a time to embrace, and a time to refrain from embracing;

a time to seek, and a time to lose;
a time to keep, and a time to throw away;
a time to tear, and a time to sew;
a time to keep silence, and a time to speak;
a time to love, and a time to hate;
a time for war, and a time for peace.

—Ecclesiastes 3:1-8

Humanist teachings

Cherish your doubts, for doubt is the attendant of truth.
Doubt is the key to the door of knowledge; it is the servant of
discovery.
A belief which may not be questioned binds us to error, for there is
incompleteness and imperfection in every belief. . . .
Let no one fear the truth, that doubt may consume it; for doubt is
a testing of belief.

—Robert T. Weston, adapted

We are of the stars,
the dust of the explosions
cast across space.

We are of the earth:
we breathe and live in the breath
of ancient plants and beasts.

We are a part
of the great circle of humanity
gathered around the fire, the
hearth, the altar.

—Joy Atkinson

Earth-centered traditions

Beauty is before me, and beauty behind me.
Above me and below me hovers the beautiful.
I am surrounded by it; I am immersed in it.
In my youth, I am aware of it,
And, in old age, I shall walk quietly the beautiful trail.
In beauty it is begun. In beauty it is ended.

    —Navajo poem

I have seen the waters flow in the river.
I have seen the flowers along the banks of the river.
Passing by, I have gazed upon the countryside
    and inhaled the perfume of orange blossoms.
I have been grateful to God and I have said thank you.

    —Algerian prayer

Guided Meditations

Inside an Egg

It is now time to settle yourself in your seat.
Relax your body.
Relax your mind.
Let the thoughts and worries in your mind melt away.
Feel your breathing.
Relax your body.

Now imagine you are very small.
You are in a safe place.
A hard shell all around you protects you.
You are inside an egg.
It is warm.
It is safe.
All your needs are taken care of.
Rest here in your egg.

This is the time for new beginnings, new life.
All around us under the ground new life is forming.
Grass, flowers, insects
are all preparing to spring forth.
There is new life approaching in the animal world, too.
The promises and excitement of the season are in the air.

Safe within your egg
you, too, are preparing to spring forth.
But first you are resting,
gathering energy you will need soon.
Spend a few moments thinking about your plans for this new year.
Is there a project you have planned?
Is there something new in your life?
Do you have a wish or a hope for this spring or summer?
While you rest, safe inside your egg,
decide on one or two things you can do to help your plan
    take shape,
your dream come true.
Take this time to rest,
to plan,
to gather the energy you will need.

The time has come. Your egg is feeling tight and cramped.
You are rested and ready to greet the world.
Stretch your arms and legs and as you emerge from your shell,
Look around you at this beautiful glorious world we live in.
Remind yourself of what you plan to do. See yourself doing it.
See in your mind your plans coming to be.

　　—Laura Wilkerson Spencer

The Light Inside You

I invite you to close your eyes and get very still and quiet.
It is very dark.
See the blackness.

Now feel the love inside you.
This love is like a light.
Feel this love and this light inside you.

And now imagine the darkness turning into sunshine.
Know that you can bring sunshine to people who are sad or
lonely or afraid.
You can bring them sunshine by sharing your love with them.
As you open your eyes
think about someone you can share your love with today.

—Colleen M. McDonald

A Ball of Color

Take a deep breath in.
Now let it out.
Deep breath in.
And out.

Keep breathing now as you think about a color.
It could be your favorite color, or a color you would like to think
    about right now.
Imagine that in your mind you can see a ball of this color.
Look at this ball.
Think about this ball.
Notice its beautiful color.

As you look at the ball in your mind you can see the ball getting
    bigger.
It is growing.
It is getting bigger and bigger and bigger until all you can see is
    the color.
It is a beautiful color.
It is all around you.
It is inside you.
It is everywhere.

Now you watch as the ball begins to shrink again.
It is getting smaller
and smaller
and smaller
until you can barely see it.
Then . . . it disappears.

   —Michelle Richards

Being in Nature

Think of your favorite spot in nature—
in a garden, in the woods, in a meadow,
by a lake, a stream or an ocean.
What does it look like?
Can you see the colors around you?
What does it sound like?
Can you hear wind or birds?
What does it smell like?
Can you smell flowers or the salt breeze?
How does being in this place make you feel?

   —Beth Casebolt

Does Your Heart Know?

As we begin our meditation, let yourself become still enough to
feel your heart beat.
Does your heart know what color your skin is?

Become quiet enough to hear your breathing.
Do your lungs care what color your skin is?

Imagine the love deep inside you
that is like a flame in your heart.
Does love care about skin color?

Know that the energy of your heartbeat,
your breathing,
and your love
is the same Energy of Life that fills all people.
We are members of one human family. Amen!

   —Colleen M. McDonald

Hush: Something's About to Happen!

Hush.
Something's about to happen.
Everything's ready.
We're poised on the edge of something. [pause]
The robins have returned.
They sing as they build nests and begin families.
Listen.
It's about to happen.
The daffodils beneath the ground have gathered up all the moisture
and the nutrients and the energy.
They are getting ready to grow.
It's about to happen.

In the Christian story of Palm Sunday,
Jesus has entered Jerusalem, a dangerous place for him.
Can you feel it?
Hush.
Something's about to happen.

In the Jewish story told this week at Passover,
Moses has told Pharaoh to "let my people go."
Will he do it?
Something's about to happen.

The chicks in their eggs are ready to break out of their shells.
Hush.
It's about to happen.
Children all over the state have gotten out their spring jackets
    and bicycles.
That first warm day is coming.
Can you feel it coming?

This week, Easter is coming.
Plans are being made—
baskets and bonnets, special foods, special decorations, all
    made ready.
Something's going to happen here.
Hush.
Can you feel it?
Do you know it,
deep down inside yourself,
that something important is coming?

This is the week to hush,
to get ready,
to know,
deep down inside,
that something wonderful will happen very soon!

This is the week to pay attention to all that is around us—
to worship with our eyes and ears and fingertips
as everything and everyone around us prepares to get ready for life
to return.

    —Gail Forsyth-Vail

The Forest Lives On

Picture yourself in a beautiful forest
with lots and lots of trees.
Some trees are young trees.
They are rather small with thin branches.
Others are very, very old trees.
Their thick trunks are huge,
Their branches very thick
As they reach up high
so high
reaching up for the sky.
You see one of these old trees
has fallen to the ground.

Sit for a moment on the trunk of this old tree.
Feel the rough bark with your fingers.
See the moss growing in the holes.
This fallen tree has become home to new life.
Life continues
in a circle.

The forest lives on
and so do we.
You hear the bubbling of a small creek
just off through the trees.
You move through the forest,
stop by the creek.
See how the water bubbles over the rocks.
See how the water flows around the sticks.
See how the water falls over the drop.
Listen to the bubbling creek.
Feel the warm sun on your cheek,
The sun that pours through the trees.
Life is all around you,

in the trees,
in the creek,
in the floor of the forest.

Life continues
in a circle.

The forest lives on
and so do we.

    —Michelle Richards

Prayers

God, give us grace to accept with serenity
the things that cannot be changed,
courage to change the things
that should be changed,
and the wisdom to distinguish
the one from the other.

    —Reinhold Niebuhr

Boundless Sea of Love and Energy, our God,
may all your dreams for us come true:
your motherly imaginings,
and your fatherly hopes,
your creative purposes everywhere in nature.
Guide us to our truest selves,
co-creators of this environment.
Make us worthy investors
of the astonishing evolutionary reality in which we live.
May it be so.

    —William Cleary, adapted

Spirit of life and spirit of grace,
Rest with us this day, in this place.
We lift up every joy, every gladness,
We hold up every hurt, every sadness
Spoken in this good company
As well as every secret feeling
Held quiet in the hollows of our hearts.

—Tess Baumberger

Be ours a religion which, like sunshine, goes everywhere;
its temple, all space;
its shrine, the good heart;
its creed, all truth;
its ritual, works of love;
its profession of faith, divine living.

—Theodore Parker

May we have eyes that see, hearts that love,
and hands that are ready to serve.

—Jackie Creuser, adapted

The inherent worth and dignity of every person

Universal Spirit of love,
O God within each one of us,
whose power reaches to the stars,
whose love connects us one to another
    and to all creation—we are one.

—Dorothy May Emerson

O God, whom we know as Love,
help us to recognize the love that surrounds us
and in which we have our being.
Help us to see ourselves as the loving people we are and can be.

—Wayne B. Arnason, adapted

I praise the blue sky.
I praise the sun that is in you.
I praise the bright moon.
I praise the shining stars in you.

—Anonymous

Justice, equity and compassion in human relations

Grant us the ability to find joy and strength
not in the strident call to arms
but in stretching out our arms
to grasp our fellow creatures
in the striving for justice and truth.

—Jewish prayer

May I become at all times, both now and forever
A protector for those without protection
A guide for those who have lost their way
A ship for those with oceans to cross
A bridge for those with rivers to cross
A sanctuary for those in danger
A lamp for those without light
A place of refuge for those who lack shelter
And a servant to all in need.

—Buddhist prayer

Acceptance of one another and encouragement to spiritual growth in our congregations

May the Spirit of Life keep you,
all that you are
and all that you are meant to become.

—Anonymous

Let our love shine forth
    from this sacred place
    that others may know
    that here they will find freedom,
    acceptance, community, and love.

—Dorothy May Emerson

Spirit of life, be present with us this hour.
Join us today as we gather in a wider search for truth and purpose.
In this quest, may we greet one another
with an open heart and mind;
May we inspire each other to consider new questions
and seek deeper meaning.
May we cultivate wisdom and compassion.
Let all who enter this sanctuary see a welcome face,
hear a kind word, and
find comfort in this community.
May all that is done and said here today
be in service to love and justice.

—Kathy Huff

A free and responsible search for truth and meaning

We believe that each individual is free to determine
    what is good and right.
Let us never forget that this freedom carries with it
    the responsibility to seek this truth.
So let us remind ourselves that this quest is important
    if we are to live a good life.
Therefore, let us reflect on the ways in which each of us
    feels called upon to change and grow.
And let us resolve that in the days and weeks to come
    we may meet this challenge.

    —Douglas Gallager, adapted

Make me strong in spirit,
Courageous in action,
Gentle of heart,

Let me act in wisdom,
Conquer my fear and doubt,
Discover my own hidden gifts,

Meet others with compassion,
Be a source of healing energies,
And face each day with hope and joy.

    —Abby Willowroot

Amid all the noise in our lives,
we take this moment to sit in silence—
    to give thanks for another day;
    to give thanks for all those in our lives who have brought us
        warmth and love;
    to give thanks for the gift of life.

We know we are on a pilgrimmage here but a brief moment in time.

Let us open ourselves, here, now,
to the process of becoming more whole—
  of living more fully;
  of giving and forgiving more freely;
  of understanding more completely
  the meaning of our lives
      here on this earth.

—Tim Haley

The right of conscience and the use of the democratic process

As I grow and learn,
help me, O Mother,
help me, O Father,
to know what is right
and to do only that.

  —Ceisiwr Serith

May all I say and all I think
  be in harmony with thee,
God within me, God beyond me,
  maker of the trees.

  —Chinook Psalter

World community, with peace, liberty and justice for all

May all the beings
in all the worlds be happy.
May all the beings
in all the worlds be happy.
May all the beings
in all the worlds be happy.
Om Peace, Peace, Peace.

—*Rig Veda*

Lord in heaven,
please listen to all those
who are praying to you now.
Those who are sad and crying,
those who have lost friends and family.
Those who are alone
and frightened.
Help them to remember
that you are there
and you are listening.

—Christian prayer

Respect for the interdependent web of all existence

Thank you for the world so sweet,
Thank you for the food we eat.
Thank you for the birds that sing.
Thank you, God, for everything.

—Christian prayer

We are thankful for the rivers and lakes—
    for the water that sustains us
We are thankful to the dirt—
    for being home to flowers and plants
We are thankful to the trees—
    for giving us air to breathe
We are thankful to the Sun—
    for the light and warmth
We are thankful to the moon—
    for giving us the tides
We are thankful to the animals—
    for all they are to us
We are thankful to the people—
    for joining us on our journey
We are thankful to our Earth
    for being our home.

   —Michelle Richards

For flowers that bloom about our feet,
for tender grass so fresh and sweet,
for song of bird and hum of bee,
for all things fair we hear or see,
Giver of all, we thank you.
For this new morning with its light,
for rest and shelter of the night,
for health and food, for love of friends,
for everything your goodness sends,
Giver of all, we thank you.

   —Anonymous, adapted

Direct experience of transcending mystery and wonder

For simple things that are not simple at all
For miracles of the common way . . .
    Sunrise . . . Sunset,
    Seedtime . . . Harvest,
    Hope . . . Joy . . . Ecstasy
For grace that turns
    our intentions into deeds
    our compassion into helpfulness
    our pain into mercy
For providence that
    sustains and supports our needs
We lift our hearts in thankfulness,
    and pray only to be more aware
    and thus more alive.

    —Gordon B. McKeeman

Let us pray to the God who holds us in the hollow of his hands,
    to the God who holds us in the curve of her arms,
to the God whose flesh is the flesh of hills and hummingbirds and
    angleworms,
whose skin is the color of an old black woman and a young white
    man, and the color of the leopard and the grizzly bear and the
    green grass snake,
whose hair is like the aurora borealis, rainbows, nebulae, waterfalls,
    and a spider's web,
whose eyes sometimes shine like the evening star, and then like
    fireflies, and then again like an open wound,
whose touch is both the touch of life and the touch of death,
and whose name is everyone's, but mostly mine.
And what shall we pray?
Let us say, "Thank you."

    —Max Coots

Words and deeds of prophetic women and men

Oh, Spirit of Life, we are grateful for our time together
   and the chance to speak the truth in love.
We are grateful for the men and women before us,
   whose prophetic words and deeds
   make our dreams possible.
We are grateful for the gift of life itself, keeping in mind
   that to respect life means both to celebrate what is
   and to insist on what it can become.
May we always rejoice in life, celebrating this precious gift,
   without forgetting that living
   also means growing and changing.
May we find in ourselves the strength to face our troubles
   and overcome them as best we can.
May we honor proudly the important people of the past,
   while keeping company with the fallen, the broken,
   and the oppressed,
     for in the dazzling heat of midday, and in the star-studded
      shimmering of night's rich blackness, we are they.

   —M. Susan Milnor, adapted

Let us remember those who came before us,
the pioneers of our faith tradition,
the architects of our denomination,
those people who've made
Unitarian Universalism what it was then
and what it is today.

   —Michelle Richards

Wisdom from the world's religions

Oh God,
You are peace.
From you comes peace,
To you returns peace.
Revive us with a salutation of peace,
And lead us to your abode of peace.

    —Islamic prayer

May I be safe
May I be happy
May I be well
May I live in peace

May you be safe
May you be happy
May you be well
May you live in peace

    —Buddhist prayer, adapted by Susan Freudenthal

Jewish and Christian teachings

God made the sun,
And God made the trees,
God made the mountains,
And God made me.
Thank you O God,
For the sun and the trees,
For making the mountains,
And for making me.

    —Christian prayer

May the words of my mouth
and the meditations of my heart
be acceptable to you
Oh Spirit of Life. . . Spirit of Love.

—Jewish prayer, adapted by Beryl Aschenberg

Humanist teachings

We believe that scientific discovery and exploring ideas
    gives life new meaning;
May we remember that there is so much yet to be discovered.
We believe that all people are worthy of respect and love
    and that together we can accomplish great things;
May we remember the responsibility is ours.

—Michelle Richards

These are the days that have been given to us;
    let us rejoice and be glad in them.
These are the days of our lives;
    let us live them well in love and service.
These are the days of mystery and wonder;
    let us cherish and celebrate them in gratitude together.
These are the days that have been given to us;
    let us make of them stories worth telling
    to those who come after us.

—William R. Murry

Earth-centered traditions

O our Father, the Sky, hear us
    and make us strong.
O our Mother, the Earth, hear us
    and give us support
O Spirit of the East,
    send us your Wisdom
O Spirit of the South,
    may we tread your path of life
O Spirit of the West,
    may we always be ready for the long journey
O Spirit of the North,
    purify us with your cleansing winds.

    —Sioux prayer

Earth mother, star mother,
You who are called by
a thousand names,
May all remember
we are cells in your body
and dance together.
You are the grain and the loaf
that sustains us each day,
And as you are patient
with our struggles to learn
So shall we be patient
with ourselves and each other.
We are radiant light
and sacred dark—the balance—
You are the embrace that heartens
And the freedom beyond fear.

Within you we are born,
we grow, live, and die—
You bring us around the circle to rebirth,
Within us you dance
Forever.

    —Starhawk

Responsive Readings and Litanies

It Matters What We Believe

Some beliefs are like walled gardens. They encourage exclusiveness, and the feeling of being especially privileged.

Other beliefs are expansive and lead the way into wider and deeper sympathies.

Some beliefs are like shadows, darkening children's days with fears of unknown calamities.

Other beliefs are like sunshine, blessing children with the warmth of happiness.

Some beliefs are divisive, separating the saved from the unsaved, friends from enemies.

Other beliefs are bonds in a universal humanity where sincere differences beautify the pattern.

Some beliefs are like blinders, shutting off the power to choose one's own direction.

Other beliefs are like gateways, opening up wide vistas for exploration.

Some beliefs weaken a person's selfhood. They blight the growth of resourcefulness.
Other beliefs nurture self-confidence and enrich the feeling of personal worth.

Some beliefs are rigid, like the body of death, impotent in a changing world.

Other beliefs are pliable, like a young sapling, ever growing with the upward thrust of life.

—Sophia Lyon Fahs

Pass It On!

Look someone right in the eye and listen to them as if they are the only one in the world at that moment. Let them know you care.

Pass it on!

Show someone a picture of something important to you.

Pass it on!

Share a passion with others—a hobby, a cause, an idea, a creative process that brings energy and joy.

Pass it on!

Show somebody how to climb a slide.

Pass it on!

Wear a big, bright smile.

Pass it on!

Hope for peaceful relations among the peoples of the world, beginning with our own actions toward those around us.

Pass it on!

Let somebody hug your teddy bear.

Pass it on!

Point out something of beauty or inspiration. Don't keep it all to yourself.

Pass it on!

Pass it on. Share the big things and the little things that make your life special. Give a piece of happiness and hope to someone, and happiness and hope will come back to you.

Pass it on! Pass it on!

—M. Maureen Killoran and Laurel Amabile

We Give Thanks

For the expanding grandeur of Creation,
worlds known and unknown,
galaxies beyond galaxies,
filling us with awe and challenging our imaginations:

We give thanks this day.

For this fragile planet earth,
its times and tides, its sunsets and seasons:

We give thanks this day.

For the joy of human life,
its wonders and surprises, its hopes and achievements:

We give thanks this day.

For our human community,
our common past and future hope,
our oneness transcending all separation,
our capacity to work for peace and justice in the midst of hostility
and oppression:

We give thanks this day.

For high hopes and noble causes, for faith without fanaticism,
for understanding of views not shared:

We give thanks this day.

For all who have labored and suffered for a fairer world,
who have lived so that others might live in dignity and freedom:

We give thanks this day.

For human liberty and sacred rites;
for opportunities to change and grow, to affirm and choose:

We give thanks this day.

We pray that we may live not by our fears but by our hopes,
not by our words but by our deeds.

—O. Eugene Pickett

We Are All Unique

We are each different. Some of us are bigger and others are smaller. Some of us are taller and others are shorter.

Our hair is different colors and our eyes are different shapes. Some of us like to spend our time playing with dinosaurs, others like playing with cards.

Some of us like running, others like reading. Some of us like eating cookies, others drinking coffee.

We are different, but we're also alike, because each of us is good at some things and not so good at others.

Each of us has days when we are kind and help others, and we each have days when we are grumpy and gruff.

We are alike because we each try to do what seems right to us. We each do the best we can.

We like it when we're happy and with good friends. But each of us has times when we are angry or sad.

Let us remember this, even though we may sometimes think life would be easier if everyone liked just what we like, and everyone thought just what we think.

Our differences are what makes each one of us unique and special.

—Axel Gerhamman

Great Spirit

Oh, Great Spirit,
whose voice I hear in the winds
and whose breath gives life to all the world, hear me.

I am small and weak.
I need your strength and wisdom.

Let me walk in beauty and make my eyes
ever behold the red and purple sunset.

Make my hands respect the things you have made
and my ears sharp to hear your voice.

Make me wise so that I may understand
the things you have taught my people.

Let me learn the lessons you have hidden
in every leaf and rock.

I seek strength, not to be superior to my brother,
but to fight my greatest enemy—myself.

Make me always ready to come to you
with clean hands and straight eyes,

so when life fades, as the fading sunset,
my spirit will come to you
without shame.

  —Chief Yellow Lark

Transitions

Life is full of transitions.
Birth begins our journey.
For the next few years,
each day is filled with awe and wonder.

In our faith, we proclaim that every night
a child is born is a holy night.
We create a safe space for exploration and discovery.

Childhood begins with our first days of school—
new friends, new experiences, a new community.

In our faith, children learn to question and to be curious. We hear
stories from around the world and we discover what makes our religion
special.

Adolescence is a time of increasing independence and responsibility
—high school, dating, driving, dances, and proms.

In our faith, youth are encouraged to lead and share responsibility for
their learning.

Young adulthood is for many the scariest, most exhilarating
period of life--high school graduation, moving away from home,
college, first job, voting, Soulful Sundown worship services.

In our faith, young adults are learning and growing in new ways,
gaining responsibilities and sharing ideas.

Adulthood is when we are to be grown up and responsible. Part-
nerships and families are created, jobs change, first homes are
purchased.

In our faith, we provide a supportive community. We help each other on our spiritual journeys through classes, discussion groups, and asking questions.

Elders are highly respected in many cultures for their wisdom, sometimes forgotten in ours—retirement, health issues, downsizing, and reaping the rewards of a life well spent.

In our faith, we support and honor our elders. We collect the stories of our elders to preserve our history and heritage.

Death—for some the end of the journey, for others the beginning of the next phase of life.

In our faith, we celebrate a life well spent through Memorial Services.

All the stages of life have a common theme—a continual journey of faith exploration and deepening spirituality.

    —Beth Casebolt, adapted

For All the Things We Know

For the things we know and the things we won't,

we light this chalice.

For questions that have answers and those that don't,

we light this chalice.

For friends who get knocked down and get up again,

we light this chalice.

We light this chalice for peace
And for friendship and love in our world.

We light this chalice.

 —M. Maureen Killoran

If There Is To Be Peace

If there is to be peace in the world,

There must be peace in the nations.

If there is to be peace in the nations,

There must be peace in the cities.

If there is to be peace in the cities,

There must be peace between neighbors.

If there is to be peace between neighbors,

There must be peace in the home.

If there is to be peace in the home,

There must be peace in the heart.

 —Lao Tse

We Light This Chalice

For every time we make a mistake
and we decide to start again,

we light this chalice.

For every time we are lonely
and we let someone be our friend,

we light this chalice.

For every time we are disappointed
and we choose to hope,

we light this, our chalice.

  —M. Maureen Killoran, adapted

Out of the Stars

Out of the stars in their flight,
out of the dust of eternity,
here we have come,
Stardust and sunlight,
mingling through time and space.

Out of the stars we have come.

Before time in the vastness of space,
earth spun to orbit the sun,
Earth with the thunder of mountains newborn, the boiling of seas.

Out of the stars we have come.

Mystery hidden in mystery,
back through all time;
Mystery rising from rocks in the storm
and the sea.

Out of the stars we have come.

Out of the stars,
rising from rocks and the sea,
kindled by sunlight on earth, arose life.

Out of the stars we have come.

This is the wonder of time;
this is the marvel of space;
out of the stars swung the earth;
life upon earth rose to love.

Out of the stars we have come.

— Robert T. Weston, adapted

Because Living Is So Dear

Why should we always be in such a hurry?

Because living is so dear.

Why are we so determined to be starved before we are hungry?

Because living is so dear.

Why must we waste so much of this life we are given with things
that just don't matter?

Because living is so dear.

I wish to learn what life has to teach.

Because living is so dear.

I do not wish to live what is not life.

Because living is so dear.
　　　—Henry David Thoreau, adapted

We Are the Light of the World

Some people say that Jesus is the light of the world. We all can be the light of the world if we seek to act in ways that enlarge the realms of love and justice.

We are the light of the world.

When we share another's pain or offer a comforting ear to a friend in need,

We are the light of the world.

When we give bread to the hungry or support ways to house the homeless,

We are the light of the world.

When we fight temptations to wrongdoing within ourselves and treat our neighbors with respect,

We are the light of the world.

When we try to overcome differences with understanding and solve conflict with peaceful means,

We are the light of the world.

When we look for the good in other people and in ourselves,

We are the light of the world.

When we do not stay quiet in the face of prejudice, but speak our minds firmly and gently,

We are the light of the world.

When we fight despair within ourselves and side with hope,

We are the light of the world.

When we use our powers justly and in the service of love for humanity,

We are the light of the world.

We are the light of the world! Amen and amen.

—Rebecca A. Edmiston-Lange, adapted

We Celebrate Our Home, the Earth

We praise the restful dark of night,
the joyous light of day!

We celebrate our home, the Earth.

We honor the water that makes the land green!

We celebrate our home, the Earth.

We care for the animals filling sea, air, and land.

We celebrate our home, the Earth.

We give thanks for this planet, for it gives us life.

We celebrate our home, the Earth.
　　　—Colleen M. McDonald

A Person Is a Puzzle

Puzzles have lots of pieces that fit together to make
a colorful picture.

A person is a puzzle.
A puzzle is a mystery we seek to solve.

Sometimes, from the inside, it feels like some pieces are missing.

A person is a puzzle.
A puzzle is a mystery we seek to solve.

We are puzzles not only to ourselves—
but to each other.

A person is a puzzle.
A puzzle is a mystery we seek to solve.

The mystery is that we are whole, even with our missing pieces.

A person is a puzzle.
A puzzle is a mystery we seek to solve.

Our missing pieces are empty spaces we might long to fill, empty spaces that make us who we are.

A person is a puzzle.
A puzzle is a mystery we seek to solve.

The mystery is that we are only what we are—and that what we are is enough.

A person is a puzzle.
A puzzle is a mystery we seek to solve.

—Mark Mosher DeWolfe, adapted

We Are Not Alone

We are not alone. We are this flame, ancient as the stars, new as the vulnerable spark.

We are not alone.

We are this chalice, rimmed by the spiral dance of searching.

We are not alone.

We are the light soaring, the shadow deepening, the dance between them.

We are not alone.

We are the heirs of the tribes and their fires, the healers and their circles.

We are not alone.

We are here. We are here for ourselves. We are here for each other. And . . .

We are not alone.

    —Michael DeVernon Boblett

Live in Me, Spirit of Life

We are alive
Because others have lived
And we all were born within homes we did not build.

Live in me, Spirit of Life.

Every one of us is alone.
No one can live a life but each self,
And we all will have made our choices before we die.

Live in me, Spirit of Life.

We are not alone.
Any act one of us will choose
must change other lives
Just as every act others choose
changes our own lives.

Live in me, Spirit of Life.

We are hurt
Most often in error
By the very risk of living
we all accept in some way.

Live in me, Spirit of Life.

Alone and bound by unbreakable bonds,
Knowing hurt and joy,
We choose to live
So that others may live,
And we may bring each other joy
And learn to salve each other's hurts.

Live in me, Spirit of Life.

—Joel Miller, adapted

We Join Our Voices in Thanks

For oceans with islands
And meadows with flowers,
Volcanoes and waterfalls,
Snowstorms and sun.

We join our voices in thanks!

For dragonflies, butterflies,
Caterpillars on leaves,
Lizards, wild turkeys, and tigers and deer,

We join our voices in thanks!

For the trees in the forest,
For acorns and rocks,
For frogs and for snakes,
For leaves and for moss,

We join our voices in thanks!

For sunset and seashells
And starfish and sand,
Octopus, jellyfish, and hammerhead shark,

We join our voices in thanks!

For the huge solar system,
The darkness of space,
For planets and starlight,
The world we all share,

We join our voices in thanks!

For horses and kitties,
Small bunnies and dogs,
For babies and family
And knowing we're loved,

We join our voices in thanks!

   —Gail Forsyth-Vail

The Rock

Though the forces of nature
push against me
they cannot break me

I am the rock
that stands firm and strong

The sun beats down on me
the wind batters me

I am the rock
that stands firm and strong

The river swells against me
tries to push me aside

I am the rock
that stands firm and strong

The forces all around me
try to break me,
but . . .

I am the rock
that stands firm and strong
  —Michelle Richards

Blessing for Friends

They live down the street,
They live far away.
We phone them, IM them,
Hang out after school.

Thanks to new friends and old friends and ones we've not met!

Friends are honest and loyal,
Kind, funny, and fun.
Friends make you feel good,
Cheer you up when you're blue.

Thanks to new friends and old friends and ones we've not met!

Sometimes we're quite different,
Maybe not the same age,
Same gender, or race,
Might not live the same way.

Thanks to new friends and old friends and ones we've not met!

We have interests in common,
We talk or we play,
We have hobbies together,
We have secrets we share.

Thanks to new friends and old friends and ones we've not met!

We make friends here at church
Where we laugh, work, or share.
We build bonds of trust
And of caring and love.

Thanks to new friends and old friends and ones we've not met!

Friends are not always perfect
And neither are we.
We get busy or grumpy
But we're loved just the same.

Thanks to new friends and old friends and ones we've not met!

—Gail Forsyth-Vail

We Open Ourselves

We come to look on beauty.

We open our eyes.

We come to sing our joy.

We open our mouths.

We come to hear of great deeds.

We open our ears.

We come to share ideas.

We open our minds.

We come to share our love.

We open our hearts.
—Colleen M. McDonald

All Things Are Connected

This we know. The earth does not belong to us; we belong to the earth.

This we know. All things are connected like the blood which unites one family.

All things are connected.

Whatever befalls the earth befalls the sons and daughters
of the earth.

We did not weave the web of life; we are merely a strand
in it.

Whatever we do to the web, we do to ourselves.
   —Chief Noah Sealth

All Things Live in Us

We live by the sun
We feel by the moon
We move by the stars

We live in all things
All things live in us

We eat from the earth
We drink from the rain
We breathe of the air

We live in all things
All things live in us

We call to each other
We listen to each other
Our hearts deepen with love and compassion

We live in all things
All things live in us

We depend on the trees and animals
We depend on the earth
Our minds open with wisdom and insight

We live in all things
All things live in us

We dedicate our practice to others
We include all forms of life
We celebrate the joy of living-dying

We live in all things
All things live in us

We are full of life
We are full of death
We are grateful for all beings and companions.

    —Stephanie Kaza

If We Love One Another

Let us love one another, because love is from God.

If we love one another, God lives in us.

Whoever does not love God
does not know God, for . . .

If we love one another, God lives in us.

No one has ever seen God.

If we love one another, God lives in us.

Those who abide in love,
abide in God,
and God abides in them.

If we love one another, God lives in us.

There is no fear in love,
for perfect love casts out fear.

If we love one another, God lives in us.

Those who say they love God but do not love their brothers and
sisters cannot love God.

If we love one another, God lives in us.

No one has ever seen God.

If we love one another, God lives in us.
   —John 4, adapted

We Have Forgotten Who We Are

We have forgotten who we are.

We have forgotten who we are.

We have alienated ourselves from the unfolding
     of the cosmos
We have become estranged from the movements
     of the earth

We have turned our backs on the cycles of life.

We have forgotten who we are.

Now the land is barren
And the waters are poisoned
And the air is polluted.

We have forgotten who we are.

Now the forests are dying
And the creatures are disappearing
And humans are despairing.

We have forgotten who we are.

We ask forgiveness
We ask for the gift of remembering
We ask for the strength to change.

We have forgotten who we are.
 —United Nations Environmental Sabbath Program, adapted

We Join with the Earth and with Each Other

We join with the earth and with each other.

To bring new life to the land
To restore the waters
To refresh the air

We join with the earth and with each other.

To renew the forests
To care for the plants
To protect the creatures

We join with the earth and with each other.

To celebrate the seas
To rejoice in the sunlight
To sing the song of the stars

We join with the earth and with each other.

To recreate the human community
To promote justice and peace
To remember our children

We join with the earth and with each other.

We join together as many and diverse expressions
of one loving mystery: for the healing of the
earth and the renewal of all life.

—United Nations Environmental Sabbath Program

Stories

Children everywhere love stories. On the next few pages, you will find several that can be used with children in worship. Each story is followed by props, responsive readings, meditations, and music that can be used in a worship service built around the theme of the story. Some discussion questions are also provided to expand the learning experience of the story.

Reflecting the Inner Light by Maria Costello O'Connor

Once upon a time there was a little pebble. You know, it was one of those in a pile among lots of other stones that looked kind of like it. They were all gray, but they all had several sides, and these sides were all a bit different, one from the other. So each pebble was unique.

And among these pebbles were lots of quartz crystals, too. These beautiful stones also had several sides, and their sides were all a bit different. But the crystals were of brilliant colors: red, orange, yellow, green, blue, purple, white. All the colors of the rainbow, plus the color white.

Now these crystals were considered the "elders" of the stone family, and the pebbles were considered the "youngers." The pebbles went to church school to learn from the crystals all the mysteries of the world. They learned about themselves and their own natures. They learned how to be in good relationship to each other and to their stone community, and they learned how to make a positive difference in the world.

One pebble was particularly curious about all these mysteries, and he asked his quartz-teacher lots and lots of questions. He wanted to know everything! Where do I come from? Who am I? What is this world?

The pebble admired one of the crystals. She was so beautiful and bright. Light seemed to shine from her and glance in colors in all directions. The pebble wanted to be like her. The crystal was a good and wise teacher and said to the pebble, "You already are shining with light, so beautiful and so bright. Just watch me, and I'll show you what I mean."

The pebble looked at the wise crystal and saw she shone with a beautiful red light. "In our rainbow principles," the teacher said, "red stands for the RESPECT that we give to each person as an individual." And they learned together about the inherent worth and dignity of every person.

Then the pebble noticed a beautiful orange light glancing from another part of the crystal. "Orange means we OFFER fair and kind treatment to all." And together they practiced justice, equity, and compassion in their relationships.

When a sparkling yellow light glanced from another of the crystal's facets, the teacher explained, "Yellow means we YEARN to learn and grow with others in our church." So they learned and practiced acceptance of one another and encouraged one another's spiritual growth.

"Now, see this green light?" said the crystal. "That means we GROW by searching freely for what is true." And in their classes they searched for truth and meaning in a free and responsible way.

"And what does that beautiful blue light that is dancing on there mean?" the little pebble asked.

"Blue means we BELIEVE in our own conscience and practice democracy," the crystal explained.

"And the purple? What is that precious purple light?"

The crystal-teacher smiled. "Purple signifies that we work for a world of PEACE and freedom for all."

The pebble was very content with all this knowledge. Together the pebble and crystal worked and played and practiced these wonderful Principles.

Then one day the pebble noticed that the crystal shone with a pure white light. The pebble was very excited. He jumped up and down and said, "I know what the white light means! I know! It means we value the interdependent WEB of life of which we are all a part!"

"That is wonderful." The crystal nodded. "You have really come a long way and have learned so much! I'm so proud!"

"Does that mean I am more like you now?" the pebble wondered. "Does that mean I can shine with light in all the colors of the rainbow?"

"Yes, it does in fact mean that," the crystal replied. "But do you see, you have always been shining with all these beautiful lights. When we have been learning about and practicing these wonderful principles, you have been learning about yourself. You see, my facets are MIRRORS. When you have looked at my colors, you have seen YOURSELF. All I have done is mirror for you who you really are."

Theme	inherent worth and dignity, seven Principles of Unitarian Universalism
Audience	preschool through adult
Props	mirror, crystals or stones of many colors
Responsive Reading	"We Open Ourselves" (page 169)
Litany	"We Are the Light of the World" (page 160)
Meditations	"The Light Inside You" (page 128)
	"UU Principles for Children" (page 113)
Hymns	"This Little Light of Mine" (*Singing the Living Tradition*, 118)

"From You I Receive" (*Singing the Living Tradition*, 402)

Questions   Who here can remember what the red crystal stands for? Orange? Yellow? Green? Blue? Purple? White?

Red stands for RESPECT. How do we show respect to other people?

Orange is for OFFERING fair and kind treatment to all. How can we be fair and kind?

Yellow means we YEARN to learn and grow with others in our church. What kinds of things do we learn here at church?

Green reminds us that we GROW by searching freely for what is true. How do we search for what is true?

Blue means we BELIEVE in our own conscience and practice democracy. Does anyone know what that means?

Purple signifies that we work for a world of PEACE and freedom for all. How can we work for peace in the world?

White is for the interdependent WEB of life. That's a really big word. Does anyone know what interdependent means?

∼

The Marvelous Loaves by Beryl Aschenberg

Grandpa Alan was a member of Nottingham Unitarian Church, and it was pretty clear that the congregation loved him. Here was a man who not only liked to bake but was also good at it. Not only that, he could always be counted on to volunteer his services for any church event that included food. Whenever he was asked about the recipe, Grandpa Alan would always state, "The secret ingredient is LOVE."

It was only natural that Grandpa Alan was asked to contribute a loaf or two to the annual Bread Communion. But Grandpa went one better—he offered to make enough of his special bread for the whole congregation to share! They all knew they were in for a treat.

When Thanksgiving rolled around, the congregation gathered. Grandpa had been baking in the church kitchen, and the building was filled with the deep yeasty fragrance of Grandpa's marvelous bread. The service began, and the minister spoke of bread—the ingredients, the process, the texture, and about the different cultures who have bread in common. And finally, it was time for the communion, or sharing of bread. The minister waved his hand to the back of the sanctuary, and Grandpa brought forward one singular, beautiful loaf. Ohhhhhhhhhhh.

Danny, a nine-year-old, was sitting in the front pew, and when Grandpa Alan came forward with just that one loaf, he couldn't help but pipe up, "How the heck are you going to feed all of us here with just one loaf of bread?"

And sure enough, the congregation started looking around and realized that there was no more coming. There were over one hundred people in that room, and the growling of stomachs was audible.

Grandpa Alan smiled as he took out the bread knife and began to slice. It was an amazing thing that happened then. Before their very eyes, the bread went "sprrrronng!," and the loaf began to multiply. Instead of one loaf, within seconds, there were twenty!

"It's a miracle!" somebody called out.

"Don't be ridiculous," Grandpa replied. "It is a sound mathematical principle."

Well, it didn't really matter what it was once everyone began eating, because it was truly the most delicious, melt-in-your-mouth bread that anyone in the whole congregation had ever tasted. What a service!

During Coffee Hour, Grandpa was approached by one member after another, thanking him for his scrumptious offering. But when Barbara moved towards him, Grandpa Alan knew that he was going to be asked for a favor. Barbara was the director of religious education.

It seemed that the youth group had been helping out at the local soup kitchen every Saturday at noon, and they were constantly running out of food to serve. There were just too many hungry people in the area.

"Alan," she asked, "can you do that trick with the bread anytime you want?"

"It really isn't a trick, Barbara," Grandpa Alan responded, "but sure, I can do it again."

They made a deal. Grandpa Alan would join the youth group at the soup kitchen with one of his marvelous loaves the following weekend.

Saturday came, and they all met up at the soup kitchen. As you can imagine, Grandpa Alan's bread was quite a hit! With so many hungry people, the loaves kept multiplying and multiplying, until every person was full and satisfied. Well, something like that doesn't stay a secret for long, and sure enough, Grandpa and his bread were one of the feature stories on the six o'clock news.

It was too bad for Grandpa Alan that on that very night, the town sheriff (yep, that's right, the Sheriff of Nottingham) was watching the news. The sheriff was not a nice person. He had been appointed to office by his brother—a man like this would NEVER have been elected. He kicked dogs, took candy from children, and swore at old folks. Not a nice bone in his body. He HATED everyone. And he was always looking for a way to get rich quick. Now, with Grandpa

Alan's marvelous bread, he figured he had a foolproof plan. He could sell loaf after loaf of bread, and it would never stop coming! All he needed was that first loaf.

So that nasty, hateful sheriff went to Grandpa Alan's house to have himself a little talk with the man. Grandpa listened as the sheriff first offered, then bargained, and then threatened, trying to get him to sell one of the marvelous loaves.

"You just don't understand," Grandpa said. "It won't work for you. Nothing personal, but there is a mathematical principle at work here."

Well, the sheriff wasn't one to take no for an answer. He pushed Grandpa out of his way, stomped into the kitchen, and grabbed the freshly baked loaf of bread that was sitting on top of the oven. Gleefully, he ran out the back door, jumped into his car, and sped home, all the while thinking about how rich he was going to be.

Once in his own kitchen, the sheriff set to work slicing the bread with a knife. He frantically sawed across the crust, and sure enough, an amazing thing happened: the bread went "sprrrronng!"

But instead of multiplying, the loaf started DIVIDING! It divided into more and more, smaller and smaller pieces, until there were just crumbs. And then even the crumbs divided, until there was nothing left at all.

Grandpa Alan had indeed known the true secret of the bread, and indeed, there was a mathematical principle that controlled it. It is actually pretty simple:

LOVE MULTIPLIES; HATRED DIVIDES.

And that is the story of Grandpa's Marvelous Loaves.

Theme	generosity and greed
Audience	preschool through adult
Prop	loaf of homemade bread

Responsive Reading	"If There Is To Be Peace" (page 157)
Meditations	"Never does hatred cease . . ." (page 115)
	"Sitting on the ground . . . " (page 115)
Hymns	"I've Got Peace Like a River" (*Singing the Living Tradition*, 100)
	"Love Will Guide Us" (*Singing the Living Tradition*, 131)
Song	"Imagine" by John Lennon
Prayer	"O God, whom we know as love . . . " (page 137)
Questions	In this story, the congregation held a bread communion. Does anyone know what a bread communion is? [*If your congregation has one, ask if anyone has been to one.*] What other types of communion do we have at our church? [*Reference flower communion, if your congregation celebrates this.*]
	Why did the loaf get smaller and smaller until there was nothing left when the sheriff stole it?
	What does it mean when we say, "Love multiplies, hate divides"?
	How does our love multiply like the loaves in this story?
	How can we show others we love them?

~

The Worry Tree by Laura Wilkerson Spencer

The family had gathered at Grandma's house for their regular Sunday dinner. As usual, it was a lively gathering with lots of talking, arguing, laughing, and joking. Eight-year-old Sarah sat quietly next to her grandmother. She ate slowly. She looked around at her family and then gave a big sigh.

"What's the matter, sweetie?" Grandma asked. "You aren't yourself tonight."

"I don't know," Sarah said.

"Are you worried about something? You look worried."

"Well, yesterday my friend Toby started playing with the new girl in class. What if she likes her better? And today Smokie" (that's her cat) "barfed all over the kitchen floor. What if he is sick? And this morning on the way to school, Dad was listening to the radio and the news sounded really scary. I thought about Cousin Mike being a soldier. What if he gets hurt?"

By this time some of the others had stopped talking and started listening to Sarah's worries. They all had worries of their own and wondered what Grandma would have to say.

"I know how you feel, Sarah," she said. "I was thinking about Mike myself. Yesterday I got a letter from my friend Brenda and she told me she was going to need surgery on her eyes. And the news sounds pretty scary to me, too, sometimes."

She looked around the table and noticed that everyone was listening now. "I have a secret trick that helps me when I am worried. I turn to a special friend when my worries get in the way of my work or make me feel bad. You see, I know that these worries don't help make things better. Holding on to my worries can keep me from making the best of each day. It can get in the way of my doing something that maybe can help."

"What's your secret trick? Who is your special friend, Grandma?" Sarah asked.

Grandma got up from the table and opened a drawer. She pulled out a pad of paper and some pens. Then she began to explain.

"When my worries are bothering me, I sit down and write them on a piece of paper. Sometimes I just write a word or two. Other times I write and write until I feel all the worries poured out onto the paper. Then I take a walk out to the back of the yard. You know that big tree way in the back corner? Grandpa planted that tree when we first moved here. I call it Grandfather Tree. Well, Grandfather Tree has a hole in it. So I take my worries and I give them to Grandfather. I put them right in the hole. I ask him to hold these worries for me. I tell them that I don't want to carry them around with me right now. It doesn't mean that I don't care about Brenda or Mike anymore. It doesn't mean what is happening on the news doesn't matter anymore. It just means that I am not weighed down. It means I can have the energy to call Brenda and write a letter to Mike. It means I am ready to go on doing what I need to do, like be your Grandma and have you all over for dinner!" She gave Sarah a little hug. "Do you want to try?"

"Yes, I do," Sarah replied. "I want to try."

"Me too," said the others.

Grandma passed around the pad of paper and each person took a piece. Soon everyone was writing. After dinner, while they were waiting for their stomachs to make room for dessert, they all took a walk to Grandfather Tree.

"Grandfather, please hold my worries for me," said Sarah. "I need some help today." Then she dropped her paper in the hole. The others did the same. They all stood there for a few moments looking at the tree, each one silently asking the tree to hold their worries.

As they walked back to the house, they all felt lighter. They stood a little straighter. They were ready to go ahead into the next day better prepared to face whatever would come their way.

Theme   worry, fear, dealing with crisis

Audience   preschool through adult

Props	pictures of trees; branch of a tree; leaves; paper and pencils; a box, can, or jar
Litany	"The Rock" (page 166)
Meditation	"For everything there is a season . . . " (page 123)
Prayers	"God, give us grace . . . " (page 135)
	"Lord in heaven, please listen . . . " (page 141)
Hymns	"Love Will Guide Us" (*Singing the Living Tradition*, 131)
	"Guide My Feet" (*Singing the Living Tradition*, 348)
	"Let It Be a Dance" (*Singing the Living Tradition*, 311)
Song	"Don't Worry, Be Happy" by Bobby McFerrin
Questions	What are some of the things you worry about?
	What do you do when you feel worried?
	Who can you talk to about things when you are worried?
	Invite participants to write down something that worries them. Fold up the paper and put it into a box, canister, or jar.

∽

The Fish Market by Christine Fry

Once upon a time, in the city of Seattle at the Pike Place Market, there was a stall that sold fish. Customers who wanted service had to work to get the attention of the men behind the counter, who were big, burly fishmongers—that's a name for people who sell fish. It wasn't always easy.

The staff seemed to work in slow motion. Picking up cold, smelly fish all day was hard, boring work. When a customer wanted to buy a fish, the fish guys used to walk from behind the counter to pick up the fish and then walk back behind the counter to wrap up the fish and ring up the purchase.

One day the new owner of the fish stall gathered the fishmongers around him. He asked for their ideas on how they could sell more fish. After a while, a young fish guy spoke up. "Hey, why don't we become world famous?"

It was a radical idea, the kind that usually comes from someone too innocent or inexperienced to know any better, but the idea took hold and grew. The fish guys discovered four important creative principles that would soon make them world famous. Show up! Choose your attitude! Play! Make people's day!

One day, soon after the meeting, one of the fishmongers walked around the counter to get a fish for a customer, but then he did something different. Instead of walking back around the counter with the fish, he threw it to one of the other guys to weigh and wrap. Whoa! Not only did this cut out a lot of walking, but it created a new form of performance. Fish were flying at the Pike Place Market.

Soon, all day long fish were being tossed over the counter by the fish guys to the delight of local shoppers and tourists from all over the world. The stall with the flying fish at the Pike Place Market did indeed become world famous, and the fish guys weren't slow and bored anymore. Their work had become play. They had a successful business plan and were even hired by other businesses to teach their workers what the fish guys had discovered.

Show up!
[*toss fish balloon out into group*]
Choose your attitude!
[*toss fish balloon out into group*]
Play!
[*toss fish balloon out into group*]
Make people's day!
[*toss fish balloon out into group and toss another one out; encourage participants to toss back and forth*]

Theme	choose your attitude
Audience	preschool through adult
Props	5 balloons (not helium) shaped like fish, 5 large rubber fish, or 5 fish-shaped stuffed toys
Litany	"Because Living Is So Dear" (page 159)
Meditation	"Finish every day . . . " (page 117)
Hymns	"Let It Be a Dance" (*Singing the Living Tradition*, 311)
	"Touch the Earth, Reach the Sky!" (*Singing the Living Tradition*, 301)
Prayer	"Boundless Sea of Love . . . " (page 135)
Questions	What does it mean to "show up"? How do you "show up"?
	What does it mean to choose your attitude? How does your attitude change the way things are?
	What are some ways you can make a person's day?
	What are your favorite ways to play? Why do you think "play" was part of their plan for success?

Mini-Sermons

The next few pages contain short sermons to use with children in worship. The sermons are accompanied by suggested props, responsive readings, prayers, and music that can be used with the sermons for a worship service built around the themes they address.

Cosmic Age by Connie Barlow

More than any other substance, our bodies are made of water. In fact, up to sixty percent of our bodies are water, and our lungs, which help us breathe, are almost ninety percent water. There just wouldn't be any me or you or [name some of the children there] without water. We are made out of water and we need water to live.

Does anyone know what the scientific name for water is?

[H_2O]

And does anyone know what the H stands for? [*hydrogen*]

Where do you suppose hydrogen comes from?

[*let students guess for a while*]

Actually, hydrogen was the first and practically only kind of atom that condensed from the hot energy that came from a huge explosion called the "Big Bang" that began the universe fourteen billion years ago. Hydrogen atoms do not live and die, like plants and animals do. So the atoms of hydrogen in this glass of water—and in your bodies right now—are all fourteen billion years old.

Now if the atoms inside you are mostly water, and if water is mostly hydrogen, and if those atoms are fourteen billion years old, how old does that make you?

Sure, you have a human age [*mention the ages of some of the children*] but you also have what's known as a "cosmic age," which connects us with the full universe. For an eight-year-old, her cosmic age would be fourteen billion and eight.

Let's take turns saying our names and our cosmic ages [*invite the children to ring a chime after their statements if one is available*].

Theme	science and reason, scientific creation story
Audience	preschool through adult
Props	a glass or bowl of water, a chime or bell
Litany	"Out of the Stars" (page 158)
Meditation	"We are of the stars . . ." (page 124)
Hymns	"Touch the Earth, Reach the Sky!" (*Singing the Living Tradition*, 301)
	"We Celebrate the Web of Life" (*Singing the Living Tradition*, 175)
Song	"Circle of Life" by Elton John

∼

Paper Bag Religion by Ruth Gibson

If the purpose of religion is to feed the spirit, then you might say it's like food we need to eat. Most of us get our food from the store. We put these groceries into a bag [*put an assortment of groceries into a bag as you continue*] and take them home, so we can feed ourselves and our loved ones with food that will be nourishing and tasty.

There are some times you might find your bag isn't big enough, or it tears, or you trip, and then you have to do some rearranging to make it all fit. Or maybe you need a bigger bag or a better bag—or you need to choose differently.

Our religion is like a bag in which we can carry all the ideas and great things that feed and sustain a healthy spirit. But what happens when our bag is already full and we need to add something to it? [*hold up a new grocery item that needs to be added to the bag—something large works best*]

It may be just a case of rearranging things in order to make the new piece fit. [*rearrange the groceries in the bag to try to make it fit*]

Or sometimes we have to take something out in order to make room for the new item we must put in our bag. [*pull one item out of the bag and set it aside*] People do this with their ideas about religion as they grow and change. Old ideas may not have the same meaning as they used to, and they need to leave in order to make room for the new ones. As Unitarian Universalists, we believe that we should learn and keep on learning all our lives. None of us has all of the answers, and sometimes our ideas about things change.

Do you have any ideas you used to think but you don't anymore? [*listen to some responses*]

That's right, we all have different ideas as we grow and change. What goes in our bag changes, too. And that's just great.

Themes	changing theology, Unitarian Universalism
Audience	preschool through adult
Props	brown paper bag and some groceries
Responsive Reading	"It Matters What We Believe" (page 149)
Litany	"For All the Things We Know" (page 156)
Meditations	"UU Principles for Children" (page 113)

	"UU Sources for Children" (page 113)
Hymns	"Enter Rejoice, and Come In" (*Singing the Living Tradition*, 361)
	"Spirit of Life" (*Singing the Living Tradition*, 123)
Songs	"The Principles Song" (page 203)
	"The Happy UU" (page 201)
	"We Are UUs" (page 202)

~

Celebrating Our Sources by Beth Casebolt

In our faith, we have seven Principles and six Sources. The Sources are the places our faith suggests that we look for answers to our questions. Remember that our faith doesn't often give us answers to our questions. Instead, each of us needs to look for the answers that feel and sound right to us. You have to choose the answer that speaks to you.

I want you to imagine a very large library. One with well-marked shelves that anyone can reach, and comfortable chairs scattered around for people to sit in, and even a small room off to one side where people can hold quiet discussions. The books of this library aren't filed by the Dewey decimal system or the Library of Congress system. Instead, they are divided into six general sections.

The first set of shelves that you find are filled with diaries and journals, pictures and videos. These are our personal experiences—and where else would you record your personal experiences but in these kinds of places? This set of shelves is unique because each person sees a different set of books and tapes. When I look, I see my diaries, journals, pictures, and videos. When you look, you see yours. And this set of shelves is always expanding and growing, because every day we have new experiences to add.

The second set of shelves is a collection of biographies, autobiographies, speeches, and writings. These works reflect the words and deeds of women and men who had important things to say about the way we should treat one another. We call them "prophetic." Some of these women and men are famous, like Dorothea Dix, Clara Barton, Ralph Waldo Emerson, William Ellery Channing, Sojourner Truth, Harriet Tubman, Abraham Lincoln, Gandhi, and Martin Luther King, Jr. Others are not—they live quietly and unknown, but they are making a difference. Some of these prophetic men and women are in our church, in our schools, and in our communities. Who are some of the prophetic women and men you know?

The wisdom of the world's religions fills the third set of shelves. Here you can find religious texts, like the Koran and the Bhagavad Gita. Writings by the leaders of the world's religions and interpretations of the texts can be found here. They are grouped by religion—Islam, Hinduism, Zoroastrianism, Buddhism, Bahaism, Sikhism, and many more.

The fourth set of shelves has Jewish and Christian texts. It may seem a little weird to have this separate from world religions, but Unitarian Universalism has a direct connection to these two faiths, making it important to separate them out and give them a special emphasis. Here we find the Bible, including all the parts that some groups include and others do not. There are the writings of many different rabbis, monks, nuns, and saints, and other religious leaders.

Science books fill a lot of our fifth set of shelves. Discoveries of science and humanist beliefs are the fifth Source. Here we find the Humanist Manifestos and other documents written by humanists, ethical statements, and the discoveries of Galileo, Isaac Newton, Maria Mitchell, Albert Einstein, Thomas Edison, Marie Curie, and others. These discoveries help us determine what is true and what is a story that helps us understand.

The last set of shelves is filled with books that teach us about the earth. We find the teachings of Native American and other earth-based religions, books about nature that study the natural rhythms in our lives, and texts about the miracle of life. We might even find a few science books here, covering topics of environmental science, biology, sexuality education, and other related fields. Off to one side, there is a small terrarium and an aquarium, since observation is one of the best ways to learn about nature.

Our Sources are like a library. In the text of the Principles and Purposes, we state that we "draw from these Sources." In other words, the Sources are where we search for the answers we seek. This is why they are important to our Unitarian Universalist faith.

Themes	UU Sources, search for truth
Audience	elementary through adult
Props	books of various types, such as autobiographies, diaries, the Bible, etc.
Litany	"For All the Things We Know" (page 156)
Meditation	"UU Sources for Children" (page 113)
Hymns	"Enter, Rejoice, and Come In" (*Singing the Living Tradition*, 361)
	"Spirit of Life" (*Singing the Living Tradition*, 123)

∿

What's in a Name? by Beryl Aschenberg

What happens when someone calls your name? [*name some of the children there*]

If you're like me, you perk up your ears and listen very hard. There may be a lot of noise in the background, like music playing or other people talking, but amidst all this, if someone says your name, you notice it.

Names are very important. Everybody has a name. If I know

your name, and someone says it, I know who they are talking about. A name is something that makes you stand out and gives people an image of who you are when they hear your name. Not only does a name tell who you are, it also says that you are a special person. I am [*your name*]—and that makes me different from you. And you are different and special as well.

But we have a problem with names sometimes, don't we? This is especially true when we meet a lot of people. We sometimes forget what their names are. Has anyone here forgotten someone's name before? What did you do? How do we solve that problem? We can begin by wanting to remember the name. It helps if we use the new name that we've learned as often as we can. Then we can take a special interest in that person. It is important that we make an extra effort to get to know people that we meet, especially in a community like our church, where we only see each other once a week or so. When we do this, we have a better chance of making friends with that person. By using people's names, we will actually be saying to them, "I know who you are, and you are important to me."

Our religion has a name too. Who can tell me the name of our religion? [*wait for responses*]

It is a unique name that tells people who we are and what we stand for. Unitarian Universalist. You may not know yet what this name means, but that is why you come to Sunday School, so that you can learn and practice being a Unitarian Universalist and all that our name means.

So as you go back to your classrooms, and as you go through the week, use each other's names often. And call each other Unitarian Universalists too—because UUs believe that everyone is important.

Theme	Unitarian Universalist identity
Audience	preschool through elementary

Prop	posterboard with *Unitarian Universalism* in large letters
Litany	"Pass it On!" (page 150)
Meditations	"UU Principles for Children" (page 113)
	"UU Sources for Children" (page 113)
Hymns	"Enter, Rejoice, and Come In" (*Singing the Living Tradition*, 361)
	"Spirit of Life" (*Singing the Living Tradition*, 123)
Song	"UU Was Its Name, Oh!" (page 203)

~

Core of Our Faith by Beth Casebolt

Umbrellas are amazing things because they fold up really small but open up really big when you need them to keep you dry.

Have you ever looked at an umbrella up close? It has lots of parts. There are little metal spines that hold onto the fabric that keeps you dry, and the handle and the part that goes up and down.

What do you think is the most important part of the umbrella? Is it the spines? If one of the spines breaks, can you still use the umbrella? Sure you can. It doesn't work quite as well, but it still works. If you get a small hole in the fabric, does it still work? You might get a little damp, but it still works. What about the handle? If the handle breaks, can you still use the umbrella? Will it still go up and down? Can you still hold it? No. The handle is pretty important, isn't it? It keeps all the parts held together so they don't fly off into space when you open it, and it keeps everything moving together when you open and close it.

Well, the umbrella is a good analogy for what we are talking about today.

The fabric is the support and protection we give each other as a community. The spines are each of us—and we are all very different, aren't we? We all believe different things, and we all have different answers to the same questions. We disagree about some things and agree about others. So, what is the handle? What keeps all of us together as a church community? Or, as we are talking about today: What is the Core of our Faith? Any ideas?

Some people believe that our seven Principles hold us together under one umbrella. Even though we all don't believe the same things, we all pretty much accept the seven Unitarian Universalist Principles as important ideas by which we should make decisions and try to live our lives. So the next time you see an umbrella, remember how it's all held together. And remember the handle that keeps all of us different people together in our faith community.

Themes	Unitarian Universalism, theological diversity, seven Principles
Audience	preschool through elementary
Prop	umbrella
Responsive Reading	"We Are All Unique" (page 153)
Litany	"We Are Not Alone" (page 163)
Meditations	"UU Principles for Children" (page 113)
	"UU Sources for Children" (page 113)
Hymns	"Enter, Rejoice, and Come In" (*Singing the Living Tradition*, 361)
	"Spirit of Life" (*Singing the Living Tradition*, 123)
Songs	"The Principles Song" (page 203)
	"The Happy UU" (page 201)

What's in Your Suitcase? by Michelle Richards

I often spend a lot of time traveling out of town, and it seems I am always trying to pack for any situation, but I still end up unprepared for the circumstances I find myself in. Spring and fall are always the hardest times of year to make those decisions about what goes in and what stays out—because it's so hard to predict what the weather is going to be like.

However, I'm learning just how important it is to pack lightly and only take with me those things that I really need. When the journey you venture upon is a spiritual one, it's not any different from other trips, even if you won't actually be going out of town. You still have to decide what things you need to take along with you.

Being a Unitarian Universalist may mean your suitcase can be a bit bigger and somewhat heavier to lug along with you on that journey, but not if you're careful about what you put into it.

You can fit a lot of great stuff into a small amount of space if you consider carefully those things you need the most. Just ask those people who go on wilderness trips with only a backpack filled with the essentials!

Being Unitarian Universalist is all about choices. No one gives you a list of what you need to bring along with you or helps you to pack everything so that it fits neatly inside your suitcase. You need to decide what to include and, perhaps more importantly, what to leave out. And you need to make sure that the things you do pack fit together with your other choices.

You may also find yourself along the road and come across something new that is important to add to your suitcase. Then you'll need to decide if you must unload something to fit this new item inside, or whether it can comfortably squeeze in.

The choices may be nearly limitless—and just like when you travel during times of unpredictable weather, you may find yourself trying to prepare for any eventuality.

But the best part of being a Unitarian Universalist is that those things that are your essential supplies may not be the same as those of any of the other people who may be accompanying you on your journey! [*Give an example of something that is spiritually meaningful to you but may not be so for others.*] So what's in your suitcase?

Themes	Unitarian Universalism, choices, theological diversity
Audience	preschool through adult
Prop	suitcase
Responsive Reading	"It Matters What We Believe" (page 149)
Meditation	"May we find within ourselves . . . " (page 117)
Hymns	"Touch the Earth, Reach the Sky!" (*Singing the Living Tradition*, 301)
	"Love Will Guide Us" (*Singing the Living Tradition*, 131)

~

A Rainbow Is a Promise by Beth Casebolt

Rainbows have lots of meanings. But the first meaning for a rainbow is a promise. Who here remembers the story of Noah and the flood from the Bible? At the end of the story, after everyone gets off the ark, the Bible tells us that God made a rainbow in the sky. God promised to never cause a flood to cover the entire earth again and that the rainbow in the sky was a symbol of this promise. Every time humans saw a rainbow, they were supposed to be reminded of God's promise to Noah.

A covenant is a type of promise. For many years, on the first day of religious education classes, you create a classroom covenant.

Does anyone remember the kinds of things that are in your covenant? What are they?

Usually your classroom covenant includes things like sharing and taking turns, no hitting or being mean, and cleaning up your own mess. In short, the covenants are promises that you, your classmates, and your teachers make to each other about how to treat each other during the religious education year. Your class covenant is also posted in the classroom for the entire year, to remind everyone in the class what they have promised. What do you do when someone new comes to the class? You show them the covenant and ask if they have any objections and, if they don't, you ask them to sign the covenant.

Anytime someone breaks the covenant, what happens? Usually someone in the class, sometimes one of the other children or youth and sometimes the teacher, points out that the covenant has been broken, and the person who broke the covenant apologizes.

So, today I want you to remember that the rainbow was the first symbol of a promise made to someone. I want you to remember that we have covenants to help us be in community together. And, next year, when our religious education year begins, you can talk about how you want to be treated in class as you create new class covenants with your classmates.

Themes	promises, covenants
Audience	preschool through elementary
Props	pictures of rainbows
Litany	"We Are Not Alone" (page 163)
Meditation	"Sitting on the ground . . . " (page 115)
Hymn	"Come, Sing a Song with Me" (*Singing the Living Tradition*, 346)
Prayer	"May the words of my mouth . . . " (page 146)
	"May we have eyes that see . . . " (page 136)

Songs

Chalice Lighting Song

Tune: "Row, Row, Row Your Boat"

Light, light, light the flame
peaceful as a dove.
Joyfully, joyfully, joyfully, joyfully
fill the world with love.

—Colleen M. McDonald

The Happy UU

Tune: "The Hokey Pokey"

You put your open mind in,
you take your open mind out,
you put your open mind in
and then you shake it all about.
You do the Happy UU and you turn the world around—
That's what it's all about!

You put your helping hands in,
you take your helping hands out,
you put your helping hands in

and then you shake them all about.
You do the Happy UU and you turn the world around —
That's what it's all about!

You put your loving hearts in,
you take your loving hearts out,
you put your loving hearts in
and then you shake them all about.
You do the Happy UU and you turn the world around—
That's what it's all about!

You put your whole self in,
don't you take yourself out.
You put your whole self in
and then you shake it all about.
You do the Happy UU and you turn the world around—
That's what it's all about!

You do the Happy UU,
you do the Happy UU,
you do the Happy UU
and then you shake it all about.
You do the Happy UU and you turn the world around—
That's what it's all about!

    —Beryl Aschenberg

We Are UUs

Tune: "We Will Rock You"

[*while singing each line, alternate between clapping twice and slapping hands on thighs*]
We are . . . we are . . . UUs!

We are . . . we are . . . loving . . .
We are . . . we are . . . learning . . .
We are . . . we are . . . helping . . .
We are . . . we are . . . UUs!

—Lori Watson

UU Was Its Name, Oh!

Tune: "B-I-N-G-O"

There were some people had a church
and UU was its name, oh.
Unitarian Universalist . . . Unitarian Universalist . . .
Unitarian Universalist,
UU was its name, oh!

—Pat Gardiner

The Principles Song

Tune: "Frère Jacques"

Respect others, Respect others,
Every one, Every one.
Everyone's important, Everyone's important,
That's number one.
That's number one.

Be fair to others, Be kind to others,
No matter who, No matter who.
Equity and kindness, Equity and kindness,
That's number two, That's number two.

In our chu-urch, In our chu-urch
[*alternative: In a U-U Con-gre-ga-tion*]
You will see, You will see.
We all search together. We accept each other.
That's number three. That's number three.

We are seeking, We are seeking
Evermore, Evermore.
Look for truth and meaning. Look for truth and meaning.
That's number four. That's number four.

Cast your ballot. Speak your mi-ind.
Do what's right. Do what's right.
Ri-ight o-of conscience, Ri-ight o-of conscience,
That's number five. That's number five.

Work for pe-eace. Work for pe-eace.
It's our fix. It's our fix.
World community-y. World community-y.
That's number six. That's number six.

All one we-eb. All one we-eb.
Say it again. Say it again.
Web of all existence. Web of all existence.
That's the end. That's the end.

    —Kathy Schroth

Closing Words

What are the ways we worship?
We worship with song and dance.
We worship with words and silence.
We worship alone and in community.
We worship in all sorts of spaces and places.
We worship with life.
Blessed Be.

—Beth Casebolt

And now may the rhythms
    of our coming together,
The melodies of our worship
And the harmonies of our farewells,
Make musical our living,
Soothing our spirits
And uplifting our souls,
This day and into the beckoning future.

—Richard S. Gilbert

We extinguish the chalice here
that it might glow gently in our hearts.
May it light your path
as you leave this place.

May it guide your way
until we are together again.

　　—Martha L. Munson

Walk softly
Speak truthfully
Love gently
Breathe deeply
Live wisely
Go in peace.

　　—Elaine Gallagher Gehrmann

Let us bless and keep one another.
Let kindness rule in our hearts
and compassion in our lives,
until we meet again. Amen.

　　—John Morgan

The inherent worth and dignity of every person

As we leave one another, let our hearts be secure through every human season.

Let our hearts be secure in times of sadness as in times of joy, in times of failure as in times of success, in times of uncertainty as in times of safety.

Let our hearts be secure in this: we are worthy of love and support, and we are worthy providers of love and support.

Let our hearts be secure, for hearts know and understand and will respond if invited in.

—James Hobart, adapted

Whatever form we are, able or disabled, rich or poor, it is not how much we do, but how much love we put in the doing—a lifelong sharing of love with others.

—Mother Teresa

Justice, equity and compassion in human relations

May we who are gathered here
be empowered by love
to weave new patterns
of Truth and Justice
into a web of life that is strong,
beautiful, and everlasting.

—Barbara W. ten Hove, adapted

In the end it won't matter
how much we have,
but how generously we have given.
It won't matter how much we know,
but rather how well we live.
And it won't matter how much we believe,
but how deeply we love.

—John C. Morgan

Acceptance of one another and encouragement to spiritual growth in our congregations

As you leave this place, take with you
A sense of joy from the gifts
   we've been honored with
A sense of appreciation
   for the work of others
   we benefit from
A sense of commitment
   to the strengthening of our church
A sense of love
   from those who support us
   in this community
And a sense of awe
   for what we can accomplish
   when we work together
   in our faith.

   —Beth Casebolt

And now may the blessings of life
be upon us and upon this congregation.
May the memories we gather here
give us hope for the future.
May the love that we share
bring strength and joy to our hearts,
and the peace of this community
be with us until we meet again.

   —Gary Kowalski

A free and responsible search for truth and meaning

Now may the love of truth guide you,
the warmth of love hold you
and the spirit of peace bless you,
this day and in the days to come.
Amen.

   —Jane E. Mauldin

To know the universe itself as a road,
as many roads,
as roads for traveling souls.

   —Walt Whitman

The right of conscience and the use of the democratic process

May words I say be fair and true
May love be a guide in all I do
May kindness sing within my heart
And may peace be with us while we're apart.

   —Beryl Aschenberg

Our time together ends.
In the days before we come together again,
may our actions match our words,
may our thoughts be filled with love,
and may we truly make a difference in a troubled world.

   —Jim Wickman

World community, with peace, liberty and justice for all

After the words, a quiet;
after the songs, a silence;
after the crowd, only the memory
    recalls the gathering.
Peace and justice have need of you
after the words, the music, and the gathering.
God grant you the depth
for dedication to justice.
God grant you the will
to be an apostle of peace.
Amen.

    —Max Coots

Go in peace,
embraced by the light
and warmth of our gathering.
Go in love,
ready again to struggle on.
Go in beauty,
shining forth like a lamp for freedom.
Amen!

    —Sarah Lammert

May the love that overcomes all differences,
    that heals all wounds,
    that puts to flight all fears,
    that reconciles all who are separated,
Be in us and among us
    now and always. Amen.

    —Frederick E. Gillis

Respect for the interdependent web of all existence

May we be connected to all things loving,
Protected from all things evil,
And guided in all ways gracious.

   —Rikkity

Deep peace of the running wave to you.
Deep peace of the flowing air to you.
Deep peace of the quiet Earth to you.
Deep peace of the shining stars to you.
Deep peace of the infinite peace to you.

   —Gaelic runes, adapted

Direct experience of transcending mystery and wonder

We will sail wild seas,
we will go where winds blow,
waves dash
and the boat speeds by under full sail.

   —Walt Whitman, adapted

The wonder everyone sees in everyone else they see, and the
wonders that fill each minute of time forever;
It is for you whoever you are—it is no farther from you than your
hearing and sight are from you.

   —Walt Whitman

Words and deeds of prophetic women and men

As we leave this place,
let us remember that those who lived before us,
who struggled for justice and suffered injustices before us,
have not melted into the dust
and have not disappeared.
They are with us still.
The lives they lived hold us steady.
We take them with us,
and with them choose the deeper path of living

    —Kathleen McTigue, adapted

Because of those who came before,
we are;
in spite of their failings,
we believe;
Because of, and in spite of the
horizons of their vision,
we, too, dream.

    —Barbara Pescan

Wisdom from the world's religions

Why do you go to the forest
in search of the Divine?
God lives in all,
and abides with you, too.
As fragrance dwells in a flower,
or reflection in a mirror,
so the Divine dwells inside everything;
seek therefore in your own heart.

    —Tegh Bahadur

Search and search again
   without losing hope;
You may find sometime
   a treasure on your way.

   —Muhammad Iqbal

Jewish and Christian teachings

Let love be genuine; hate what is evil, hold fast to what is good.

   —Romans 12:9

Let your light so shine
that all may see
and Rejoice
that you are.

   —Matthew 5:16, adapted by Byrd Tetzlaff

Sing songs as you go, and hold close together. You may at times grow confused and lose your way. . . . Touch each other and keep telling the stories.

   —Alla Renee Bozarth

Humanist teachings

We are made of stardust
every single atom
of carbon and of oxygen, calcium and iron.

   —Connie Barlow

We now go forth
on our journey
through an ever-expanding
and ever-changing universe
whose truths are always unfolding
and whose nature
we are only beginning to understand.

—Michelle Richards

Earth-centered traditions

Grandfather Great Spirit
Fill us with the light
Give us the strength to understand and the eyes to see.
Teach us to walk the soft earth as relatives
To all that live.

—Sioux prayer

Blessing of green plants, blessing of forests:
Cedar, douglas fir, swordfern, salal bush.
Blessing of fish and birds, blessing of mammals:
Salmon, eagle, cougar, and mountain goat.
May all humankind likewise offer blessing...
Bless the wisdom of the holy one above us;
Bless the truth of the holy one beneath us;
Bless the love of the holy one within us.

—Chinook psalter

Orders of Service

The following samples demonstrate how to incorporate various service elements into a cohesive program of worship.

Inner Light

Goals   instill a sense of UU Identity with a ritual involving the seven Principles

communicate ideas about diverse images of the divine by presenting different types of prayers during each worship

explore guided meditation techniques

create a climate of generosity by taking a collection

Chalice Lighting   Barbara J. Pescan (page 105)

Hymn   "This Little Light of Mine"
(*Singing the Living Tradition*, 118)

Ritual Lighting of Rainbow Candles

Prayer   Wayne Arnason (page 137)

Guided Meditation	"The Light Inside You" Colleen M. McDonald (page 128)
Story	"Reflecting the Inner Light" Maria Costello O'Connor (page 175)
Litany	"We Are Not Alone" Michael DeVernon Boblett (page 163)
Collection	"From You I Receive" (*Singing the Living Tradition*, 402)
Closing Words	Sarah Lammert (page 210)

We Are All Connected

Goals	create a sense of community through the sharing of joys and concerns
	celebrate the specialness of life by lifting our voices in song
	explore spiritual practices such as prayer and meditation

Opening Music	nature sounds from a relaxation CD
Chalice Lighting	Walt Whitman (page 107)
Sharing of Joys and Concerns	
Guided Meditation	"The Forest Lives On" Michelle Richards (page 133)

Hymn	"Spirit of Life" (*Singing the Living Tradition*, 123)
Story	"All I See Is Part of Me" Chara Curtis (see page 227)
Responsive Reading	"All Things Are Connected" adapted from Chief Noah Sealth (page 169)
The Web of Life Activity	*Children stand in a circle. One child throws a ball of yarn to another child while holding onto one end. The child who catches it holds onto the thread and tosses the ball to someone else. Continue until the children have created a web of yarn between them.*
Hymn	"We Celebrate the Web of Life" (*Singing the Living Tradition*, 175)
Meditation	Algerian prayer (page 125)
Closing Hymn	"As We Leave This Friendly Place" (*Singing the Living Tradition*, 414)

Transcendent Mystery and Wonder

Goals   create a sense of community experiencing spiritual growth together

offer opportunities for children to express themselves creatively and spiritually

explore the spiritual practices of many religions

Opening Music	"Spring" Vivaldi
Chalice Lighting	Michelle Richards (page 108)
Hymn	"Spirit of Life" (*Singing the Living Tradition*, 123)
Litany	"Live in Me, Spirit of Life" Joel Miller (page 164)
Spiritual Practice	*Tai Chi* (*to sound of meditative music*)
Meditation	Deuteronomy 33:13–16 (page 121)
Hymn	"Gathered Here" (*Singing the Living Tradition*, 389) *Pass out rhythm instruments and* *encourage the group to create a* *pleasing sound together.*
Closing Words	"The wonder everyone sees … " Walt Whitman (page 211)

For More Information and Ideas

General

Brown, Carolyn. *You Can Preach to the Kids, Too: Designing Sermons for Children and Adults.* Nashville, TN: Abington Press, 1997.

Cavaletti, Sophia. *The Religious Potential of the Child.* New York: Paulist Press, 1983.

Coles, Robert. *The Spiritual Life of Children.* Boston: Houghton Mifflin, 1990.

Commission on Common Worship. *Leading Congregations in Worship: A Guide.* Boston: Unitarian Universalist Association of Congregations, 1983.

Cox, Meg. *The Book of New Family Traditions: How to Create Great Rituals for Holidays and Everyday.* Philadelphia: Running Press, 2003.

Crowley, Abby, et al. *Windmills, Worship and Wonder.* Waldorf, MD: Greater Washington Association Religious Education Council, 1996.

Dougy Center for Grieving Children. *35 Ways to Help a Grieving Child.* Portland, OR: The Dougy Center for Grieving Children, 2004.

Essex Conversations Coordinating Committee, ed. *Essex Conversations: Visions for Lifespan Religious Education.* Boston: Skinner House Books, 2001.

Fowler, James. *Stages of Faith: The Psychology of Human Development and the Quest for Meaning*. San Francisco: HarperSanFrancisco, 1981.

Gardner, Howard. *Frames of Mind: The Theory of Multiple Intelligences*. New York: Harper & Row, 1983.

Nieuwejaar, Jeanne Harrison. *The Gift of Faith: Tending the Spiritual Lives of Children*. Boston: Skinner House Books, 2002.

Procession: Engaging Worship Matters for the Next Generation. Chicago: Evangelical Lutheran Church of America, May 2001.

Rizzuto, Anna Maria. *The Birth of the Living God*. Chicago: University of Chicago Press, 1979.

Sylvia, Ron. *Starting High Definition Churches*. Oscala, FL: High Definition Resources, 2004.

Stonehouse, Catherine. *Joining Children on the Spiritual Journey: Nurturing a Life of Faith*. Grand Rapids, MI: Baker Books, 1998.

Tieger, Paul D., and Barbara Barron-Tieger. *Nurture by Nature*. Toronto: Little, Brown, 1997.

Tobias, Cynthia Ulrich. *The Way They Learn*. Carol Stream, IL: Tyndale House Publishers, 1994.

Wallerstein, Judith, Julia Lewis, and Sandra Blakeslee. *The Unexpected Legacy of Divorce*. New York: Hyperion, 2000.

Meditation

Bretherten, Barbara Ann. *Prayer Themes and Guided Meditations for Children*. New London, CT: Twenty-Third Publications, 1998.

Carbone, Christopher Kavi. *Namaste! Songs, Yoga & Meditations for Young Yogis*. Newport, RI: Arts in Celebration, 2005.

Desmond, Lisa. *Baby Buddhas: A Guide for Teaching Meditation to*

Children. Riverside, NJ: Andrews McMeel Publishing, 2004.

Edelman, Marian Wright. *Guide My Feet: Prayers and Meditations for Our Children*. Boston: Beacon Press, 1995.

Felix, Antonia. *Prayers & Meditations for Children*. New York: Smithmark Publishers, 1997.

Fontana, David. *Teaching Meditation to Children: A Practical Guide to the Use and Benefits of Meditation Techniques*. Boston: Element Books, 1998.

Garth, Maureen. *Earthlight: New Meditations for Children*. San Francisco: HarperSanFrancisco, 1997.

_____. *Moonbeam: A Book of Meditations for Children*. Melbourne: CollinsDove, 1992.

_____. *Sunshine: More Meditations for Children*. Melbourne: CollinsDove, 1994.

_____. *Starbright: Meditations for Children*. San Francisco: HarperSanFrancisco, 1991.

Halpin, Marlene. *The Ball of Red String: A Guided Meditation for Children*. Chicago: Loyola Press, 1998.

Harper, Sally. *Teach the Children Meditation*. Austin, TX: First World Library, 2003.

Hendricks, Gay, and Russel Wills. *The Centering Book: Awareness Activities for Children, Parents, and Teachers*. New York: Prentice Hall Press, 1975.

Hendricks, Gay, and Thomas B. Roberts. *The Second Centering Book: More Awareness Activities for Children & Adults to Relax the Body & Mind*. New York: Prentice Hall Press, 1977.

Hendricks, Gay. *The Family Centering Book: Awareness Activities the Whole Family Can Do Together*. Upper Saddle River, NJ: Prentice-Hall Press, 1979.

Pappas, Michael G. *Sweet Dreams for Little Ones: Bedtime Fantasies to Build Self-Esteem.* San Francisco: Harper & Row, 1982.

Payne, Lauren Murphy. *Just Because I Am: A Child's Book of Affirmation.* Hong Kong: Free Spirit Publishing, 1994.

Pickett, Helen, ed. *Rejoice Together: Prayers, Meditations, and Other Readings For Family, Individual and Small Group Worship.* Second edition. Boston: Skinner House, 2006.

Redfield, Salle Merrill. *The Joy of Meditating.* New York: Warner Books, 1995.

Reehorst, Jane. *Guided Meditations for Children.* Orlando, FL: Harcourt, 2000.

Roberts, Elizabeth, and Elias Amidon. *Earth Prayers: 365 Prayers, Poems and Invocations for Honoring the Earth.* San Francisco: HarperSanFrancisco, 1991.

_____. *Life Prayers: 365 Prayers, Blessings and Affirmations to Celebrate the Human Journey.* San Francisco: HarperSanFrancisco, 1996.

Rozman, Deborah. *Meditating with Children: The Art of Concentration and Centering.* Boulder Creek, CA: University of the Trees Press, 1975.

Viegas, Marneta. *The Wishing Star: 52 Meditations for Children.* Berkeley, CA: O Books, 2004.

Storybooks

The inherent worth and dignity of every person

Adoff, Arnold. *Black Is Brown Is Tan.* New York: Amistad Press, 2004.

Andrae, Giles. *Giraffes Can't Dance.* London, UK: Orchard Books, 2007.

Blume, Judy. *The One In the Middle Is a Green Kangaroo*. New York: Atheneum/Richard Jackson, 1982.

de Paola, Tomie. *Now One Foot, Now the Other*. New York: Putnam Juvenile, 2005.

_____. *Oliver Button Is a Sissy*. New York: Harcourt Brace Jovanovich/Voyager Books, 1979.

DeRolf, Shane. *The Crayon Box That Talked*. New York: Random House, 1997.

Dooley, Norah. *Everybody Bakes Bread*. Minneapolis: Carolrhoda Books, 1995.

_____. *Everybody Brings Noodles*. Minneapolis: Carolrhoda Books, 2002.

_____. *Everybody Cooks Rice*. Boston: Houghton Mifflin, 1995.

_____. *Everybody Serves Soup*. Minneapolis: Carolrhoda Books, 2000.

Emmett, Jonathan. *Ruby in Her Own Time*. New York: Scholastic, 2007.

Freeman, Don. *Dandelion*. Pine Plains, NY: Live Oak Media, 2005.

Friedman, Ina. *How My Parents Learned to Eat*. Orlando, FL: Harcourt, 1991.

Knowles, Sheena. *Edward the Emu*. New York: HarperTrophy, 1998.

Henkes, Kevin. *Chester's Way*. New York: HarperTrophy, 1997.

_____. *Chrysanthemum*. New York: Scholastic, 2005.

Lionni, Leo. *The Biggest House in the World*. New York: Dragonfly Books, 1973.

_____. *A Color of His Own*. New York: Knopf Books, 2006.

_____. *Little Blue and Little Yellow*. New York: HarperTrophy, 1995.

Maguire, Arlene. *We're All Special*. Santa Monica, CA: Portunus Publishing, 1998.

McPhail, David. *Something Special*. New York: Little, Brown, 1992.

Palocco, Patricia. *Just Plain Fancy*. New York: Bantam Doubleday Dell, 1994.

_____. *The Keeping Quilt*. New York: Aladdin , 2001.

_____. *The Trees of the Dancing Goats*. New York: Aladdin, 2000.

Parr, Todd. *It's Okay To Be Different*. New York: Little, Brown, 2004.

Seuss, Dr. *Horton Hears a Who*. New York: Random House, 1990.

_____. "The Sneeches," in *The Sneetches and Other Stories*. New York: Random House, 1961.

Spier, Peter. *People*. Royal Oak, MI: Echo Publications, 2000.

Steig, William. *Amos & Boris*. New York: Farrar, Straus & Giroux, 1992.

Yarborough, Camille. *Cornrows*. New York: Putnam Juvenile, 1997.

Zolotow, Charlotte. *Some Things Go Together*. New York: Harper-Festival, 1999.

Justice, equity and compassion in human relations

Adoff, Arnold. *Black Is Brown Is Tan*. New York: Amistad Press, 2004.

Bradby, Marie. *Momma, Where Are You From?* London, UK: Orchard Books, 2000.

Coleman, Evelyn. *White Socks Only*. Morton Grove, IL: Albert Whitman & Co., 1999.

Demi. *One Grain of Rice: A Mathematical Folktale*. New York: Scholastic, 1997.

de Paola, Tomie. *Now One Foot, Now the Other.* New York: Putnam Juvenile, 2005.

Henkes, Kevin. *Lilly's Purple Plastic Purse.* New York: Greenwillow Books, 2001.

Hoffman, Mary. *Amazing Grace.* Hayes, Middlesex, UK: Magi Publications, 2000.

Johnson, D.B. *Henry Climbs a Mountain.* Boston: Houghton Mifflin, 2003.

Lionni, Leo. *A Color of His Own.* New York: Knopf Books, 2006.

McGovern, Anne. *Stone Soup.* New York: Scholastic, 1986.

McPhail, David. *The Teddy Bear.* New York: Henry Holt, 2005.

Newman, Leslea. *Heather Has Two Mommies.* Los Angeles: Alyson Publications, 2000.

Rice, David L. *Because Brian Hugged His Mother.* Nevada City, CA: Dawn Publications, 1999.

Roehe, Stephanie. *That's Not Fair.* New York: Minedition, 2004.

Seuss, Dr. *Horton Hears a Who.* New York: Random House, 1990.

_____. "The Sneetches," in *The Sneetches and Other Stories.* New York: Random House, 1961.

_____. "Yertle the Turtle," in *Yertle the Turtle and Other Stories.* New York: Random House, 1958.

Willhoite, Michael. *Daddy's Roommate.* Los Angeles: Alyson Publications, 1991.

_____. *Daddy's Wedding.* Los Angeles: Alyson Publications, 1996.

Acceptance of one another and encouragement to spiritual growth

Aliki. *The Two of Them.* New York: HarperTrophy, 1987.

Barner, Bob. *To Everything.* San Francisco: Chronicle Books, 2004.

Bedard, Michael. *Emily.* New York: Dragonfly Books, 2002.

Bulla, Clyde. *Daniel's Duck.* New York: HarperTrophy, 1982.

Chin-Lee, Cynthia. *Almond Cookies and Dragon Well Tea.* Chicago: Polychrome Publishing, 1993.

de Paola, Tomie. *The Knight and the Dragon.* New York: Putnam Juvenile, 1998.

_____. *Oliver Button Is a Sissy.* New York: Harcourt Brace Jovanovich/Voyager Books, 1979.

_____. *Watch Out for Chicken Feet in Your Soup.* New York: Simon & Schuster, 1974.

DeRolf, Shane. *The Crayon Box That Talked.* New York: Random House, 1997.

Everitt, Betsy. *Mean Soup.* Orlando, FL: Harcourt Brace, 1992.

Fair, Sylvia. *The Bedspread.* London: Pan MacMillan, 1986.

Freeman, Don. *Dandelion.* Pine Plains, NY: Live Oak Media, 2005.

Friedman, Ina. *How My Parents Learned To Eat.* New York: Harcourt, 1991.

Gold, Phyllis-Terri. *Please Don't Say Hello.* New York: Human Sciences Press, 1986.

Henkes, Kevin. *Owen.* New York: Greenwillow Books, 1993.

Leaf, Munro. *The Story of Ferdinand.* New York: Grosset & Dunlap, 2000.

Lionni, Leo. *Frederick.* New York: Alfred A. Knopf, 1967.

_____. *Little Blue and Little Yellow*. New York: HarperTrophy, 1995.

Miles, Miska. *Annie and the Old One*. New York: Trumpet Club, 1990.

Munsch, Robert. *The Paper Bag Princess*. New York: Scholastic, 2003.

_____. *Love You Forever*. Glens Falls, NY: Red Fox Books, 2001.

Polacco, Patricia. *Thank You, Mr. Falker*. New York: Philomel, 2001.

Sasso, Sandy Eisenberg. *God Said Amen*. Woodstock, VT: Jewish Lights Publishing, 2000.

Seuss, Dr. *Bartholemew and the Oobleck*. New York: Random House, 1980.

_____. "The Sneetches," in *The Sneetches and Other Stories*. New York: Random House, 1961.

_____. *Oh, the Thinks You Can Think*. New York: Random House, 1975.

Zolotow, Charlotte. *The Quarreling Book*. New York: HarperTrophy, 1982.

A free and responsible search for truth and meaning

Andersen, Hans Christian. *The Emperor's New Clothes*. Boston: Houghton Mifflin, 2004.

Boritzer, Etan. *What Is God?* Willowdale, ON: Firefly Books, 1990.

Carle, Eric. *The Tiny Seed*. New York: Aladdin, 1990.

Curtis, Chara. *All I See Is Part of Me*. Bellevue, WA: Illumination Arts Publishing, 1994.

de Paola, Tomie. *The Knight and the Dragon.* New York: Putnam Juvenile, 1998.

Domanska, Janina. *What Do You See?* Boston: Macmillan, 1974.

Fisher, Aileen. *I Stood Upon a Mountain.* New York: T.Y. Crowell, 1979.

Johnson, D.B. *Henry Hikes to Fitchburg.* Boston: Houghton Mifflin, 2006.

Knowles, Sheena. *Edwina the Emu.* New York: HarperTrophy, 1997.

Matthews, Caitlin. *The Blessing Seed: A Creation Myth for the New Millennium.* Cambridge, MA: Barefoot Books, 2000.

Munsch, Robert. *The Paper Bag Princess.* New York: Scholastic, 2003.

Muth, John. *The Three Questions.* New York: Scholastic, 2003.

_____. *Zen Shorts.* New York: Scholastic, 2005.

Neasi, Barbara. *Listen to Me.* New York: Children's Press, 2002.

Polacco, Patricia. *The Bee Tree.* New York: Putnam Juvenile, 1998.

Seuss, Dr. *Horton Hears a Who.* New York: Random House, 1990.

_____. *Oh, the Thinks You Can Think.* New York: Random House, 1975.

Silverstein, Shel. *The Missing Piece.* New York: HarperCollins, 1976.

Thaler, Mike. *Owly.* New York: Walker Books, 1998.

Varley, Susan. *Badger's Parting Gifts.* New York: HarperTrophy, 1992.

Williams, Jay. *Everyone Knows What a Dragon Looks Like.* New York: Aladdin, 1984.

Williams, Margery. *The Velveteen Rabbit*. New York: Avon, 1999.

Wood, Douglas. *Grandad's Prayers of the Earth*. Cambridge, MA: Candlewick Press, 1999.

Zolotow, Charlotte. *The Hating Book*. New York: HarperTrophy, 1989.

_____. *The Storm Book*. New York: HarperTrophy, 1989.

The right of conscience and the use of the democratic process

Bradby, Marie. *Momma, Where Are You From?* London, UK: Orchard Books, 2000.

Brott, Ardyth. *Jeremy's Decision*. Minneapolis: Tandem Library, 1996.

Burns Knight, Margy. *Who Belongs Here? An American Story*. Gardiner, ME: Tilbury House, 1996.

Brumbeau, Jeff. *The Quiltmaker's Gift*. New York: Scholastic, 2001.

Cronin, Doreen. *Click, Clack, Moo! Cows That Type*. New York: Simon & Schuster, 2003.

_____. *Duck for President*. New York: Simon & Schuster, 2004.

Demi. *The Empty Pot*. New York: Henry Holt, 1996.

McPhail, David. *The Teddy Bear*. New York: Henry Holt, 2005.

Millman, Dan. *The Secret of the Peaceful Warrior*. Tiburon, CA: HJ Kramer Starseed Press, 1992.

Quinlan, Patricia. *Planting Seeds*. Toronto: Annick Press, 1996.

Seuss, Dr. *Bartholemew and the Oobleck*. New York: Random House, 1980.

_____. "King Louie Katz," in *I Can Lick Thirty Tigers Today!* New York: Random House, 1980.

_____."Yertle the Turtle," in *Yertle the Turtle and Other Stories*. New York: Random House, 1958.

World community, with peace, liberty and justice for all

Boone-Jones, Margaret. *Martin Luther King, Jr.: A Picture Story*. New York: Children's Press, 1968.

Bulla, Clyde Robert. *The Poppy Seeds*. New York: Puffin, 1994.

Coles, Robert. *The Story of Ruby Bridges*. New York: Scholastic, 2004.

de Paola, Tomie, *The Knight and the Dragon*. New York: Putnam Juvenile, 1998.

DiSalvo-Ryan, Dyanne. *Uncle Willie and the Soup Kitchen*. New York: HarperTrophy, 1997.

Hamanaka, Sheila. *Peace Crane*. New York: HarperCollins, 1995.

Hopkinson, Deborah. *Sweet Clara and the Freedom Quilt*. New York: Knopf Books, 2003.

Leaf, Munro. *The Story of Ferdinand*. New York: Grosset & Dunlap, 2000.

Lobel, Anita. *Potatoes, Potatoes*. New York: Greenwillow Books, 2004.

MacDonald, Margaret Read. *Peace Tales*. Atlanta: August House, 2005.

McPhail, David. *The Teddy Bear*. New York: Henry Holt, 2005.

Millman, Dan. *The Secret of the Peaceful Warrior*. Tiburon, CA: HJ Kramer Starseed Press, 1992.

Muth, John J. *The Three Questions*. New York: Scholastic, 2003.

Polacco, Patricia. *Chicken Sunday*. New York: Putnam Juvenile, 1998.

_____. *Pink and Say*. New York: Philomel, 1994.

Quinlan, Patricia. *Planting Seeds*. Toronto: Annick Press, 1996.

Seuss, Dr. *The Butter Battle Book*. New York: Random House, 1984.

_____. *Horton Hears a Who*. New York: Random House, 1990.

_____. *What Was I Scared Of?* New York: Random House, 1997.

_____. "Yertle the Turtle," in *Yertle the Turtle and Other Stories*. New York: Random House, 1958.

Zolotow, Charlotte. *The Hating Book*. New York: HarperTrophy, 1989.

_____. *The Quarreling Book*. New York: HarperTrophy, 1982.

Respect for the interdependent web of all existence

Atwood, Margaret. *For the Birds*. Ontario: Firefly Books, 1991.

Baylor, Byrd. *The Desert Is Theirs*. New York: Aladdin, 1987.

_____. *Everybody Needs a Rock*. New York: Aladdin, 1985.

_____. *Hawk, I'm Your Brother*. New York: Atheneum, 1976.

_____. *The Way to Start a Day*. New York: Aladdin, 1986.

Boritzer, Etan. *What Is Love?* Santa Monica, CA: Veronica Lane Books, 1996.

Carle, Eric. *The Tiny Seed*. New York: Aladdin, 1990.

Cooney, Barbara. *Miss Rumphius*. New York: Puffin, 1985.

Curtis, Chara. *All I See Is Part of Me*. Bellevue, WA: Illumination Arts Publishing, 1994.

DeMunn, Michael. *Places of Power*. Nevada City, CA: Dawn Publications, 1997.

Ehlert, Lois. *Red Leaf, Yellow Leaf*. New York: Harcourt, 1998.

Ets, Marie Hall. *Play With Me*. New York: Puffin, 1976.

Haskell-Leger, Diane. *Maxine's Tree*. Custer, WA: Orca Book Publishers, 1990.

Jeffers, Susan. *Brother Eagle, Sister Sky*. New York: Dutton Books, 1993.

Kinsey-Warnock, Natalie. *The Bear That Heard Crying*. New York: Scholastic, 1998.

Langstaff, John. *Over in the Meadow*. New York: Puffin, 1999.

McCloskey, Robert. *Make Way for Ducklings*. New York: Puffin, 1999.

Morris, Martha. *Katherine and the Garbage Dump*. Toronto: Second Story Press, 1993.

Rand, Gloria, and Ted Rand. *Prince William*. New York: Henry Holt, 1994.

Romanova, Natalie. *Once There Was a Tree*. New York: Puffin, 1992.

Rylant, Cynthia. *Every Living Thing*. New York: Aladdin, 1988.

Seuss, Dr. *Horton Hears a Who*. New York: Random House, 1990.

_____. *The Lorax*. New York: HarperCollins, 2004.

Thornhill, Jan. *A Tree in a Forest*. Toronto: Maple Tree Press, 1991.

Udry, Janice May. *A Tree Is Nice*. New York: HarperTrophy, 1987.

Wood, Douglas. *Grandad's Prayers of the Earth*. Cambridge, MA: Candlewick Press, 1999.

Yolen, Jane. *Owl Moon*. New York: Philomel, 1987.

Zolotow, Charlotte. *The Storm Book*. New York: HarperTrophy, 1989.

Direct experience of transcending mystery and wonder

Anthony, Joseph. *The Dandelion Seed*. Nevada City, CA: Dawn Publications, 1997.

Barron, T.A. *Where Is Grandpa?* New York: Putnam Juvenile, 2001.

Bea, Holly. *Where Does God Live?* Tiburon, CA: HJ Kramer Starseed Press, 1992.

Baylor, Byrd. *Hawk, I'm Your Brother*. New York: Atheneum, 1976.

Boritzer, Etan. *What Is God?* Willowdale, ON: Firefly Books, 1990.

Boroson, Martin. *Becoming Me: A Story of Creation*. London, UK: Frances Lincoln, 2002.

Brown, Margaret Wise. *The Dead Bird*. New York: William Morrow, 2007.

Carle, Eric. *Papa, Please Get the Moon for Me*. New York: Simon & Schuster, 1991.

_____. *The Very Hungry Caterpillar*. New York: Black Butterfly Children's Books, 1994.

Curtis, Chara. *All I See Is Part of Me*. Bellevue, WA: Illumination Arts Publishing, 1994.

Curtis, Jamie Lee. *Tell Me Again About the Night I Was Born*. New York: HarperTrophy, 2000.

DeMunn, Michael. *Places of Power*. Nevada City, CA: Dawn Publications, 1997.

Ehlert, Lois. *Red Leaf, Yellow Leaf.* New York: Harcourt, 1998.

Fisher, Aileen. *I Stood Upon a Mountain.* New York: T.Y. Crowell, 1979.

Frasier, Debra. *On the Day You Were Born.* New York: Harcourt, 2005.

Fowler, Susi Gregg. *When Joel Comes Home.* New York: Greenwillow Books, 1993.

Gelmann, Mark. *Does God Have a Big Toe?* New York: HarperTrophy, 1993.

Gerstein, Mordicai. *The Mountains of Tibet.* New York: HarperTrophy, 1989.

Goble, Paul. *Beyond the Ridge.* New York: Aladdin, 1993.

Gold, August. *Where Does God Live?* Tiburon, CA: HJ Kramer Starseed Press, 1992.

Grigg, Carol. *The Great Change.* Hillsboro, OR: Beyond Words Publishing, 1992.

Hanh, Thich Nhat. *A Pebble for Your Pocket.* Berkeley, CA: Plum Blossom Books, 2002.

Hanson, Warren. *The Next Place.* Golden Valley, MN: Waldman House Press, 1997.

Hathorn, Libby. *Grandma's Shoes.* New York: Little, Brown, 1994.

Kushner, Lawrence, and Karen Kushner. *Because Nothing Looks Like God.* Woodstock, VT: Jewish Lights Publishing, 2000.

Lewis, Debra Shaw. *When You Were a Baby.* Atlanta: Peachtree Publishers, 1995.

Lindahl, Kay. *How Does God Listen?* Woodstock, VT: Skylight Path Publishing, 2005.

Martignacco, Carole. *The Everything Seed: A Story of Beginnings*. Berkeley, CA: Ten Speed Press, 2006.

Mellonie, Bryan. *Lifetimes: A Beautiful Way to Explain Death to Children*. New York: Bantam Books, 1983.

Miles, Miska. *Annie and the Old One*. New York: Trumpet Club, 1990.

Mills, Joyce. *Gentle Willow: A Story for Children About Dying*. Washington, DC: Magination Press, 2003.

Moore, Mary Ann. *Hide-and-Seek with God*. Boston: Skinner House Books, 2005.

Rosen, Michael. *We're Going on a Bear Hunt*. New York: Aladdin, 2003.

Sasso, Sandy Eisenberg. *God's Paintbrush*. Woodstock, VT: Jewish Lights Publishing, 2004.

_____. *In God's Name*. Woodstock, VT: Jewish Lights Publishing, 1994.

_____. *For Heaven's Sake*. Woodstock, VT: Jewish Lights Publishing, 1999.

Shulevitz, Uri. *Rain Rain Rivers*. New York: Farrar, Straus & Giroux, 2006.

Steig, William. *Amos & Boris*. New York: Farrar, Straus & Giroux, 1992.

Tichnor, Richard, and Jenny Smith. *A Spark in the Dark*. Nevada City, CA: Dawn Publications, 1997.

Varley, Susan. *Badger's Parting Gifts*. New York: HarperTrophy, 1992.

Viorst, Judith. *The Tenth Good Thing About Barney*. New York: Aladdin, 1987.

Williams, Margery. *The Velveteen Rabbit*. New York: Avon, 1999.

Wirth, Victoria. *Whisper from the Woods*. New York: Simon & Schuster, 1991.

Wood, Douglas. *Grandad's Prayers of the Earth*. Cambridge, MA: Candlewick Press, 1999.

_____. *Old Turtle*. New York: Scholastic, 2007.

Yolen, Jane. *Owl Moon*. New York: Philomel, 1987.

Zolotow, Charlotte. *The Storm Book*. New York: HarperTrophy, 1989.

Words and deeds of prophetic women and men

Boone-Jones, Margaret. *Martin Luther King, Jr.: A Picture Story*. New York: Children's Press, 1968.

Davidson, Margaret. *I Have a Dream: The Story of Martin Luther King, Jr.* New York: Scholastic, 1991.

Johnson, D.B. *Henry Builds a Cabin*. Boston: Houghton Mifflin, 1991.

_____. *Henry Climbs a Mountain*. Boston: Houghton Mifflin, 2003.

_____. *Henry Hikes to Fitchburg*. Boston: Houghton Mifflin, 2006.

Lasky, Kathryn. *She's Wearing a Dead Bird on Her Head*. New York: Hyperion Books, 1997.

Wisdom from the world's religions

Bouchard, David. *Buddha in the Garden*. Vancouver, BC: Raincoast Books, 2002.

Buice, Christopher. *A Bucketful of Dreams*. Boston: Skinner House Books, 1994.

Conover, Sarah. *Kindness: A Treasury of Buddhist Wisdom*. Spokane, WA: Eastern Washington University Press, 2001.

Demi. *Buddha Stories*. New York: Henry Holt, 1997.

_____. *The Empty Pot*. New York: Henry Holt, 1996.

_____. *One Grain of Rice: A Mathematical Folktale*. New York: Scholastic, 1997.

de Paola, Tommie. *The Legend of the Persian Carpet*. New York: Putnam Juvenile, 1993.

Gerstein, Mordicai. *The Mountains of Tibet*. New York: Harper-Trophy, 1989.

Hanh, Thich Nhat. *A Pebble for Your Pocket*. Berkeley, CA: Plum Blossom Books, 2002.

Kimmel, Eric. *The Three Princes: A Tale from the Middle East*. New York: Holiday House, 2000.

Shepard, Alan. *Forty Fortunes: A Tale of Iran*. New York: Clarion Books, 1999.

Shepard, Alan. *The Enchanted Storks: A Tale of the Middle East*. New York: Clarion Books, 1995.

Jewish and Christian teachings

Barner, Bob. *To Everything*. San Francisco: Chronicle Books, 2004.

de Paola, Tomie. *The Parables of Jesus*. New York: Holiday House, 1995.

_____. *Mary: Mother of Jesus*. New York: Holiday House, 1995.

Gelmann, Mark. *Does God Have a Big Toe?* New York: Harper-Trophy,1993.

Lester, Julius. *When the Beginning Began.* Orlando, FL: Silver Whistle/Harcourt Brace, 1999.

Matthews, Caitlin. *The Blessing Seed: A Creation Myth for the New Millennium.* Cambridge, MA: Barefoot Books, 2000.

Palocco, Patricia. *The Trees of the Dancing Goats.* New York: Aladdin, 2000.

Humanist teachings

de Paola, Tomie. *Strega Nona.* New York: Putnam Juvenile, 2000.

Frasier, Debra. *On the Day You Were Born.* Orlando, FL: Harcourt, 2005.

Martignacco, Carole. *The Everything Seed: A Story of Beginnings.* Berkeley, CA: Ten Speed Press, 2006.

Munsch, Robert. *The Paper Bag Princess.* New York: Scholastic, 2003.

Seuss, Dr. *Bartholemew and the Oobleck.* New York: Random House, 1980.

_____. *Oh, the Thinks You Can Think.* New York: Random House, 1975.

Tichnor, Richard, and Jenny Smith, *A Spark in the Dark.* Nevada City, CA: Dawn Publications, 1997.

Earth-centered traditions

Baylor, Byrd. *The Desert Is Theirs.* New York: Aladdin, 1987.

Casler, Leigh. *The Boy Who Dreamed of an Acorn*. New York: Philomel, 2001.

Curtis, Chara. *All I See Is Part of Me*. Bellevue, WA: Illumination Arts Publishing, 1994.

Chief Seattle and Susan Jeffers. *Brother Eagle, Sister Sky: A Message from Chief Seattle*. New York: Dutton Books, 1993.

Cherry, Lynn. *The Great Kapok Tree: A Tale of the Amazon Rainforest*. Orlando, FL: Voyager/Harcourt, 2000.

DeMunn, Michael, *Places of Power*. Nevada City, CA: Dawn Publications, 1997.

Romanova, Natalie. *Once There Was a Tree*. New York: Puffin, 1992.

Rylant, Cynthia. *Every Living Thing*. New York: Aladdin, 1988.

Shulevitz, Uri. *Rain Rain Rivers*. New York: Farrar, Straus & Giroux, 2006.

Wood, Douglas. *Old Turtle*. New York: Scholastic, 2007.

Story Collections

Buice, Christopher. *A Bucketful of Dreams*. Boston: Skinner House Books, 1994.

Caduto, Michael. *Earth Tales from Around the World*. Golden, CO: Fulcrum Publishing, 2006.

Carle, Eric. *Stories for All Seasons*. New York: Simon & Schuster, 1998.

Cole, Joanna. *Best-Loved Folktales of the World*. New York: Anchor Books, 1983.

Conover, Sarah. *Kindness: A Treasury of Buddhist Wisdom for Children and Parents.* Spokane, WA: Eastern Washington University Press, 2001.

_____. *Taking Flight: A Book of Story Meditations.* New York: Doubleday, 1988.

Fahs, Sophia Lyon. *From Long Ago and Many Lands: Stories for Children Told Anew,* Second Edition. Boston: Skinner House Books, 1995.

Forest, Heather. *Wisdom Tales from Around the World.* Little Rock, AR: August House, 1996.

Gelmann, Mark. *Does God Have a Big Toe?* New York: Harper-Trophy, 1993.

Grohsmeyer, Janeen. *A Lamp in Every Corner: Our Unitarian Universalist Storybook.* Boston: Unitarian Universalist Association of Congregations, 2004.

Hammer, Randy. *Everyone a Butterfly: 40 Sermons for Children.* Boston: Skinner House Books, 2004.

Hanh, Thich Nhat. *A Pebble for Your Pocket.* Berkeley, CA: Plum Blossom Books, 2002.

Haven, Kendall. *New Year's to Kwanzaa: Original Stories of Celebration.* Golden, CO: Fulcrum Publishing, 1999.

Holt, David. *More Ready-to-Tell Tales from Around the World.* Little Rock, AR: August House, 2000.

_____. *Ready-to-Tell Tales.* Little Rock, AR: August House, 1994.

Jordan, Jerry Marshall. *One More Brown Bag.* Cleveland, OH: Pilgrim Press, 1983.

Lester, Julius. *When the Beginning Began.* Orlando, FL: Silver Whistle/Harcourt Brace, 1999.

MacDonald, Margaret. *Peace Tales*. Little Rock, AR: August House, 1992.

McDonald, Colleen M. *What If Nobody Forgave? And Other Stories*. Boston: Skinner House Books, 2002.

Moore, Mary Ann. *Hide-and-Seek with God*. Boston: Skinner House Books, 2005.

Muth, John J. *Zen Shorts*. New York: Scholastic, 2005.

Ross, Jeanette. *Telling Our Tales: Stories and Storytelling for All Ages*. Boston: Skinner House Books, 2002.

Seuss, Dr. *Yertle the Turtle and Other Stories*. New York: Random House, 1958.

Thomas, Marlo. *Free to Be You and Me*. Cambridge, MA: Running Press, 2002.

Williams, Arlene. *Tales from the Dragon's Cave*. Sparks, NV: Waking Light Press, 1996.

Williams, Betsy Hill. *UU & Me!: Collected Stories*. Boston: Skinner House Books, 2003.

Child-Friendly Hymns

May This Light Shine: A Songbook for Children and Youth. Charlotte, NC: UU Musicians Network, 2006.

Now Let Us Sing! Songs for All Ages, compiled and arranged by Phyllis Robbins. Kingston, ON: Kingston Unitarian Press, 2004.

Singing the Living Tradition, Boston: Unitarian Universalist Association, 1993:

8   Mother Spirit, Father Spirit

38   Morning Has Broken

100   I've Got Peace Like a River

104   When Israel Was in Egypt's Land

116   I'm On My Way

118   This Little Light of Mine

121   We'll Build a Land

123   Spirit of Life

128   For All That Is Our Life

131   Love Will Guide Us

134   Our World Is One World

167   Nothing but Peace is Enough

168   One More Step

169   We Shall Overcome

170   We Are a Gentle, Angry People

175   We Celebrate the Web of Life

188   Come, Come, Whoever You Are

191   Now I Recall My Childhood

211   We Are Climbing Jacob's Ladder

212   We Are Dancing Sarah's Circle

220   Bring Out the Festal Bread

301   Touch the Earth, Reach the Sky!

311   Let It Be a Dance

338   I Seek the Spirit of a Child

346   Come, Sing a Song with Me

348   Guide My Feet

361   Enter, Rejoice, and Come In

384   Alleluia

387   The Earth, Water, Fire, Air

389   Gathered Here

395   Sing and Rejoice

397   Morning Has Come

402   From You I Receive

407   We're Gonna Sit at the Welcome Table

413   Go Now in Peace

414   As We Leave This Friendly Place

Singing the Journey, Boston: Unitarian Universalist Association, 2005:

1002   Comfort Me

1007   There's a River Flowin' in My Soul

1010   Where Do We Come From?

1011   Return Again

1018   Come and Go with Me

1020   Woyaya

1023   Building Bridges

1024   When the Spirit Says Do

1034   Siyahamba

1040   Hush

1053   How Could Anyone

Multicultural Resources

Books

Kidwell, Clara Sue, et al. *A Native American Theology.* Maryknoll, NY: Orbis Books, 2001.

Smith, Huston. *The World's Religions.* New York: HarperOne, 1991.

Takaki, Ronald. *A Different Mirror: A History of Multicultural America.* Boston: Back Bay Publishing, 1994.

Zinn, Howard. *A Peoples' History of the United States.* New York: Harper Perennial, 2005.

Websites

Digital History, **www.digitalhistory.uh.edu**
Hypertext American history textbook with links to primary sources, as well as an "Ethnic Voices" section, which includes Asian American, Native American, Mexican American, and Enslaved Voices.

Diversity Database, University of Maryland
www.magenta.nl/crosspoint
Comprehensive index of multicultural and diversity resources.

Encyclopediamythica, **www.pantheon.org**
Exhaustive resource for researching the mythology, folklore, and religions of the world. Click on the region you are interested in,

then the religion or people, and you will find an alphabetical list of entries on the culture's pantheons and myths.

History World, **www.historyworld.net**
Searchable and indexed to help you research and learn about cultures around the world.

Interfaith Calendar, **www.interfaithcalendar.org**
Includes calendars for the current year and years ahead. Each calendar lists sacred days for world religions and offers definitions and explanations for the holy days. Also included are links to information on different religions and spiritual practices.

Kidipede, History for Kids, **www.historyforkids.org**
Lets children click on links to various regions—West Asia, India, North America, and Africa included—to learn about ancient cultures. Further links describe each culture's art, food, environment, religion, and more. Separate links for Islam and for the Middle Ages are also included. Each of these pages also recommends books on the subjects they display.

National Geographic, **www.nationalgeographic.com**
Easy online atlas to the world. Click on "People and Places" and browse a long list of links to countries, regions, and cities for facts, feature articles, and beautiful photography.

Official Denominational Websites
http://hirr.hartsem.edu/denom/homepages.html
Allows you to go straight to the source and learn about a plethora of American religious sects in their own words. Created and maintained by the Hartford Institute for Religion Research.

Smithsonian Institute for Folklife and Cultural Heritage
www.folklife.si.edu
Online exhibits with beautiful photo-documentation. Links to Smithsonian Global Sound music archive allow you to listen to traditional native music, contemporary regional songs, and spoken word from around the world.

Time for Kids, **www.timeforkids.com**
Click on "Around the World" and find links to different countries, with fun tools like "native lingo," which has audio files and pronunciation keys for saying "hello," "thank you," and more in different languages. Each country has a clickable "sightseeing guide" and facts and figures. After learning about a particular country, kids can send an e-postcard to tell friends what they have learned.

United Religious Initiative, **www.uri.org**
An interfaith, peace-building global community whose members include people from over 65 countries practicing over 100 religions and indigenous traditions. Click on the "Kid's Site" link to find kid-friendly descriptions of these religious traditions as well as activities, games, and songs.

Acknowledgments

I would like to thank the following people who submitted their creative resources upon my request: Beryl Aschenberg, Beth Casebolt, Betsy Darr, Gail Forsyth-Vail, Rev. Christine Fry, Rev. Ruth Gibson, Rev. Colleen M. McDonald, Maria Costello O'Connor, Laura Wilkerson Spencer, and Rev. Elizabeth Strong. Thanks also to all the people who sent me lists of their congregation's goals and sample orders of service: Beryl Aschenberg, Karen Brown, Betsy Darr, Leia Durland-Jones, Betty Skwarek, Jolinda Stephens, Kathy Underwood, Terry Ward, and Patty Withers. I would also like to thank Beth Brownfield, Elizabeth Katzmann, and Rev. Ruth Gibson for the information they gave me on how the Principles came to be paired with the colors of the rainbow.

Thanks also to Rev. Gordon Gibson, my colleague of many years and partner in planning worship services. Certainly I need to thank the children of the Unitarian Universalist Fellowship of Elkhart for the years they spent reaching for rainbows with me and their parents for allowing me to do so. Last, but certainly not least, I would also like to acknowledge the tireless efforts of those people who spent hours poring over multiple drafts and whose suggestions made this work stronger because of the input I received: Rev. Randy Becker, Patty French, and Bryan Richards.

251